D0946509

VIETNAMESE IMMIGRATION

Joe Ferry

THE CHANGING
Face of North America:
IMMIGRATION SINCE 1965

VIETNAMESE
IMMIGRATION

Joe Ferry

MASON CREST PUBLISHERS
PHILADELPHIA

Produced by OTTN Publishing, Stockton, New Jersey

Mason Crest Publishers
370 Reed Road
Broomall, PA 19008
www.masoncrest.com

First printing

1 3 5 7 9 8 6 4 2

Library of Congress Cataloging-in-Publication Data

Ferry, Joseph.
  Vietnamese immigration / Joe Ferry.
     p. cm. — (The changing face of North America)
Summary: An overview of immigration from Vietnam to the United States and Canada since the 1960s, when United
States troops entered the controversial Vietnamese Conflict and war refugees sought to escape persecution.
Includes bibliographical references and index.
  ISBN 1-59084-682-6
1. Vietnamese Americans—History—20th century—Juvenile literature. 2. Vietnamese—Canada—History—20th
century—Juvenile literature. 3. Immigrants—United States—History—20th century—Juvenile literature.
4. Immigrants—Canada—History—20th century—Juvenile literature. 5. Vietnam—Emigration and immigration—
History—20th century—Juvenile literature. 6. United States—Emigration and immigration—History—20th
century—Juvenile literature. 7. Canada—Emigration and immigration—History—20th century—Juvenile literature.
[1. Vietnamese Americans—History—20th century. 2. Vietnamese—Canada—History—20th century.
3. Immigrants—United States—History—20th century. 4. Immigrants—Canada—History—20th century.
5. Vietnam—Emigration and immigration—History—20th century. 6. United States—Emigration and immigration—History—20th century. 7. Canada—Emigration and immigration—History—20th century.] I. Title. II. Series.
  E184.V53F47 2004
  304.8'730597—dc22
                                                                                    2003016372

THE CHANGING
Face of North America:
IMMIGRATION SINCE 1965

CONTENTS

INTRODUCTION

THE CHANGING FACE OF AMERICA

By Senator Edward M. Kennedy

America is proud of its heritage and history as a nation of immigrants, and my own family is an example. All eight of my great-grandparents were immigrants who left Ireland a century and a half ago, when that land was devastated by the massive famine caused by the potato blight. When I was a young boy, my grandfather used to take me down to the docks in Boston and regale me with stories about the Great Famine and the waves of Irish immigrants who came to America seeking a better life. He talked of how the Irish left their marks in Boston and across the nation, enduring many hardships and harsh discrimination, but also building the railroads, digging the canals, settling the West, and filling the factories of a growing America. According to one well-known saying of the time, "under every railroad tie, an Irishman is buried."

America was the promised land for them, as it has been for so many other immigrants who have found shelter, hope, opportunity, and freedom. Immigrants have always been an indispensable part of our nation. They have contributed immensely to our communities, created new jobs and whole new industries, served in our armed forces, and helped make America the continuing land of promise that it is today.

The inspiring poem by Emma Lazarus, inscribed on the pedestal of the Statue of Liberty in New York Harbor, is America's welcome to all immigrants:

Give me your tired, your poor,
Your huddled masses yearning to breathe free,
The wretched refuse of your teeming shore,
Send these, the homeless, tempest-tossed, to me:
I lift my lamp beside the golden door.

The period since September 11, 2001, has been particularly challenging for immigrants. Since the horrifying terrorist attacks, there has been a resurgence of anti-immigrant attitudes and behavior. We all agree that our borders must be safe and secure. Yet, at the same time, we must safeguard the entry of the millions of persons who come to the United States legally each year as immigrants, visitors, scholars, students, and workers. The "golden door" must stay open. We must recognize that immigration is not the problem—terrorism is. We must identify and isolate the terrorists, and not isolate America.

One of my most important responsibilities in the Senate is the preservation of basic rights and basic fairness in the application of our immigration laws, so that new generations of immigrants in our own time and for all time will have the same opportunity that my great-grandparents had when they arrived in America.

Immigration is beneficial for the United States and for countries throughout the world. It is no coincidence that two hundred years ago, our nations' founders chose *E Pluribus Unum*—"out of many, one"—as America's motto. These words, chosen by Benjamin Franklin, John Adams, and Thomas Jefferson, refer to the ideal that separate colonies can be transformed into one united nation. Today, this ideal has come to apply to individuals as well. Our diversity is our strength. We are a nation of immigrants, and we always will be.

FOREWORD

THE CHANGING FACE OF THE UNITED STATES

Marian L. Smith, historian
U.S. Immigration and Naturalization Service

Americans commonly assume that immigration today is very different than immigration of the past. The immigrants themselves appear to be unlike immigrants of earlier eras. Their language, their dress, their food, and their ways seem strange. At times people fear too many of these new immigrants will destroy the America they know. But has anything really changed? Do new immigrants have any different effect on America than old immigrants a century ago? Is the American fear of too much immigration a new development? Do immigrants really change America more than America changes the immigrants? The very subject of immigration raises many questions.

In the United States, immigration is more than a chapter in a history book. It is a continuous thread that links the present moment to the first settlers on North American shores. From the first colonists' arrival until today, immigrants have been met by Americans who both welcomed and feared them. Immigrant contributions were always welcome—on the farm, in the fields, and in the factories. Welcoming the poor, the persecuted, and the "huddled masses" became an American principle. Beginning with the original Pilgrims' flight from religious persecution in the 1600s, through the Irish migration to escape starvation in the 1800s, to the relocation of Central Americans seeking refuge from civil wars in the 1980s and 1990s, the United States has considered itself a haven for the destitute and the oppressed.

But there was also concern that immigrants would not adopt American ways, habits, or language. Too many immigrants might overwhelm America. If so, the dream of the Founding Fathers for United States government and society would be destroyed. For this reason, throughout American history some have argued that limiting or ending immigration is our patriotic duty. Benjamin Franklin feared there were so many German immigrants in Pennsylvania the Colonial Legislature would begin speaking German. "Progressive" leaders of the early 1900s feared that immigrants who could not read and understand the English language were not only exploited by "big business," but also served as the foundation for "machine politics" that undermined the U.S. Constitution. This theme continues today, usually voiced by those who bear no malice toward immigrants but who want to preserve American ideals.

Have immigrants changed? In colonial days, when most colonists were of English descent, they considered Germans, Swiss, and French immigrants as different. They were not "one of us" because they spoke a different language. Generations later, Americans of German or French descent viewed Polish, Italian, and Russian immigrants as strange. They were not "like us" because they had a different religion, or because they did not come from a tradition of constitutional government. Recently, Americans of Polish or Italian descent have seen Nicaraguan, Pakistani, or Vietnamese immigrants as too different to be included. It has long been said of American immigration that the latest ones to arrive usually want to close the door behind them.

It is important to remember that fear of individual immigrant groups seldom lasted, and always lessened. Benjamin Franklin's anxiety over German immigrants disappeared after those immigrants' sons and daughters helped the nation gain independence in the Revolutionary War. The Irish of the mid-1800s were among the most hated immigrants, but today we all wear green on St. Patrick's Day. While a century ago it was feared that Italian and other Catholic immigrants would vote as directed by the Pope, today that controversy is only a vague memory. Unfortunately, some ethnic groups continue their efforts to earn acceptance. The African

Americans' struggle continues, and some Asian Americans, whose families have been in America for generations, are the victims of current anti-immigrant sentiment.

Time changes both immigrants and America. Each wave of new immigrants, with their strange language and habits, eventually grows old and passes away. Their American-born children speak English. The immigrants' grandchildren are completely American. The strange foods of their ancestors—spaghetti, baklava, hummus, or tofu—become common in any American restaurant or grocery store. Much of what the immigrants brought to these shores is lost, principally their language. And what is gained becomes as American as St. Patrick's Day, Hanukkah, or Cinco de Mayo, and we forget that it was once something foreign.

Recent immigrants are all around us. They come from every corner of the earth to join in the American Dream. They will continue to help make the American Dream a reality, just as all the immigrants who came before them have done.

FOREWORD

THE CHANGING FACE OF CANADA

Peter A. Hammerschmidt
First Secretary, Permanent Mission of Canada to the United Nations

Throughout Canada's history, immigration has shaped and defined the very character of Canadian society. The migration of peoples from every part of the world into Canada has profoundly changed the way we look, speak, eat, and live. Through close and distant relatives who left their lands in search of a better life, all Canadians have links to immigrant pasts. We are a nation built by and of immigrants.

Two parallel forces have shaped the history of Canadian immigration. The enormous diversity of Canada's immigrant population is the most obvious. In the beginning came the enterprising settlers of the "New World," the French and English colonists. Soon after came the Scottish, Irish, and Northern and Central European farmers of the 1700s and 1800s. As the country expanded westward during the mid-1800s, migrant workers began arriving from China, Japan, and other Asian countries. And the turbulent twentieth century brought an even greater variety of immigrants to Canada, from the Caribbean, Africa, India, and Southeast Asia.

So while English- and French-Canadians are the largest ethnic groups in the country today, neither group alone represents a majority of the population. A large and vibrant multicultural mix makes up the rest, particularly in Canada's major cities. Toronto, Vancouver, and Montreal alone are home to people from over 200 ethnic groups!

Less obvious but equally important in the evolution of Canadian immigration has been hope. The promise of a better life lured Europeans and Americans seeking cheap (sometimes even free) farmland. Thousands of Scots and Irish arrived to escape grinding poverty and starvation. Others came for freedom, to escape religious and political persecution. Canada has long been a haven to the world's dispossessed and disenfranchised—Dutch and German farmers cast out for their religious beliefs, black slaves fleeing the United States, and political refugees of despotic regimes in Europe, Africa, Asia, and South America.

The two forces of diversity and hope, so central to Canada's past, also shaped the modern era of Canadian immigration. Following the Second World War, Canada drew heavily on these influences to forge trailblazing immigration initiatives.

The catalyst for change was the adoption of the Canadian Bill of Rights in 1960. Recognizing its growing diversity and Canadians' changing attitudes towards racism, the government passed a federal statute barring discrimination on the grounds of race, national origin, color, religion, or sex. Effectively rejecting the discriminatory elements in Canadian immigration policy, the Bill of Rights forced the introduction of a new policy in 1962. The focus of immigration abruptly switched from national origin to the individual's potential contribution to Canadian society. The door to Canada was now open to every corner of the world.

Welcoming those seeking new hopes in a new land has also been a feature of Canadian immigration in the modern era. The focus on economic immigration has increased along with Canada's steadily growing economy, but political immigration has also been encouraged. Since 1945, Canada has admitted tens of thousands of displaced persons, including Jewish Holocaust survivors, victims of Soviet crackdowns in Hungary and Czechoslovakia, and refugees from political upheaval in Uganda, Chile, and Vietnam.

Prior to 1978, however, these political refugees were admitted as an exception to normal immigration procedures. That year, Canada

revamped its refugee policy with a new Immigration Act that explicit-
ly affirmed Canada's commitment to the resettlement of refugees
from oppression. Today, the admission of refugees remains a central
part of Canadian immigration law and regulations.

Amendments to economic and political immigration policy
continued during the 1980s and 1990s, refining further the bold
steps taken during the modern era. Together, these initiatives have
turned Canada into one of the world's few truly multicultural states.

Unlike the process of assimilation into a "melting pot" of cultures,
immigrants to Canada are more likely to retain their cultural identity,
beliefs, and practices. This is the source of some of Canada's
greatest strengths as a society. And as a truly multicultural nation,
diversity is not seen as a threat to Canadian identity. Quite the
contrary—diversity *is* Canadian identity.

1 THE VIETNAMESE IN NORTH AMERICA

The last quarter of the 20th century brought about significant changes to the population of North America, as millions of people migrated from around the world to the United States and Canada. One of the most sudden and significant flows of migration came from a tiny country located on the extreme southeastern tip of Asia—Vietnam.

As a result of that migration, the number of people of Vietnamese descent living in North America now stands at more than one million. The U.S. Census, a survey of the nation's population taken every 10 years, indicated that in 2000 there were 1.1 million Vietnamese people living in the United States. The Canadian census showed that as of 2001 there were more than 148,000 people of Vietnamese descent living in Canada. In both countries the Vietnamese represent one of the fastest-growing Asian groups.

People of Asian descent come from countries of the Far East, Southeast Asia, or the Indian subcontinent (these three regions include Cambodia, China, India, Japan, Korea, Malaysia, Pakistan, the Philippine Islands, Thailand, and Vietnam). Of the more than 280 million Americans living in the United States in 2000, almost 12 million reported having an Asian background (about 4.2 percent of the U.S. population). People of Vietnamese descent living in the United States account for about 10 percent of the Asian American population.

◄ Vietnamese refugees aboard a freighter wait to go ashore, 1979. Since the 1970s the United States and Canada have accepted tens of thousands of Vietnamese refugees, who today make up a large segment of the Vietnamese living in North America.

Asians in the United States and Canada

The U.S. Census Bureau did not use "Asian" as a category in recording people's ethnic backgrounds until the latter half of the 1800s. At that time, most Asian immigrants came from China or Japan. By the beginning of the 1900s, additional Asian categories also recorded people who came from the Philippine Islands and Korea. However, it was not until the 1980 census that "Vietnamese" became a category, in response to the growth in immigration from Vietnam that occurred after 1975.

The influx of immigrants from Asia to North America is a

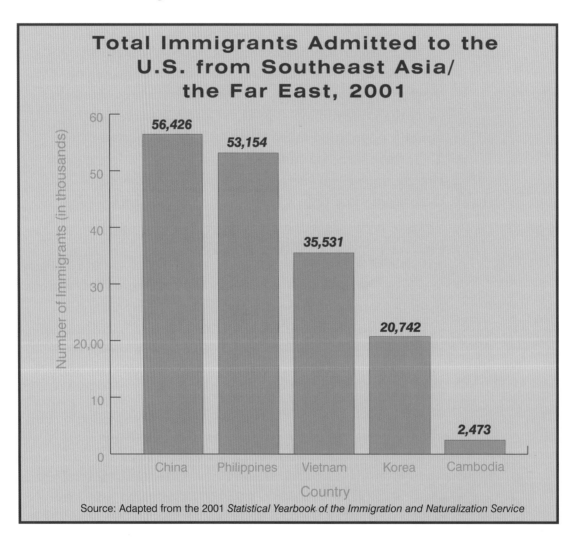

Total Immigrants Admitted to the U.S. from Southeast Asia/ the Far East, 2001

Number of Immigrants (in thousands)

- China: 56,426
- Philippines: 53,154
- Vietnam: 35,531
- Korea: 20,742
- Cambodia: 2,473

Country

Source: Adapted from the 2001 *Statistical Yearbook of the Immigration and Naturalization Service*

recent phenomenom. In 1970, according to the U.S. Census no Asian nations were among the 10 countries sending the most foreign-born immigrants to the United States (as determined by their birthplace, or "place of origin"). Yet in 2000, five Asian countries were on this list—China, India, Korea, the Philippines, and Vietnam.

From 1990 to 2000, the Vietnamese population in the United States almost doubled in size, growing from 593,213 to 1,122,528, according to the U.S. Census. Today it is the third-largest Asian group, after the Chinese and Filipinos, entering the United States. One indication of the growing presence of people from this Southeast Asian country was the U.S. Census 2000 forms—Vietnamese was one of the four languages that was used in the census questions.

Of the 29.6 million people living in Canada in 2001, according to the Canadian census, almost 2 million are of Asian background. The Vietnamese population of 148,000 makes up 8 percent of Canada's Asian population.

The Vietnamese in North America

According to U.S. Census records, relatively few Vietnamese lived in North America before 1975. Figures from 1951 to 1960 indicate that only 335 Vietnamese lived in the United States, and only 150 lived in Canada. Almost all were college and university students.

Then, in the early 1960s, after the United States entered a controversial war in Vietnam, the numbers of Vietnamese immigrating to North America began to rise. During the 1960s about 4,000 Vietnamese came to U.S. shores. By 1970 approximately 10,000 Vietnamese were living in the United States. During that time Vietnamese migration to Canada increased slightly as well, resulting in a Vietnamese population of about 1,200 by 1970.

In the decade that followed, these numbers rose dramatically. During the 1970s, most Vietnamese entered North America as refugees seeking to escape persecution in their country. From

1970 to 1974 the number of people of Vietnamese descent living in North America grew to about 14,500, then reached just over 18,000 by the next year. This was followed by a major surge of Vietnamese migration, from 1975 to 1980, when tens of thousands fled to North America.

Altogether almost a half a million people, or an average of 100,000 Vietnamese immigrants per year, entered the United States during the latter part of the 1970s. The average yearly numbers of Vietnamese migration dropped somewhat during the 1980s and 1990s, but it continued at a steady pace thereafter.

Since the 1970s, on average between 25,000 and 40,000 Vietnamese per year have come to North America. In just three decades, this large-scale immigration has increased the Vietnamese presence in North America from a few hundred to more than a million.

The Vietnamese People

Vietnamese immigrants have come from both remote agricultural regions and fast-paced cities of Vietnam. About 85 percent of them are descended from the Kinh, or Viet, tribe from southern China and from people of the Indonesian islands. They speak one of three dialects of Vietnamese, depending upon whether they are from the northern, central, or southern region of the country. However, the dialects are similar enough to be understood by nearly all Vietnamese. The majority of ethnic Vietnamese have lived as rice farmers in villages located along the seacoast or river regions.

Another 12 percent of the Vietnamese are Khmers (farmers and fishermen who came originally from Cambodia) or Montagnards (the French word for "mountain people"). The Montagnards are members of hill tribes such as the Hmong, Yao, Meo, Nung, Thai, and Jarai ethnic groups, who speak different languages and dialects. About 3 percent of Vietnam's population consists of ethnic Chinese, who have traditionally worked as merchants in urban areas.

Most Vietnamese follow the Buddhist faith, but several other

Many Vietnamese immigrants have left behind an agricultural life. In Vietnam farming in the river and coastal regions is a common source of income.

world religions are practiced in Vietnam, including Christianity, Hinduism, and Islam, as well as combinations of some of these religions.

Influence on Western Culture

As their numbers have increased over the past few decades, the Vietnamese have impacted the food, arts, and society of their new homeland in many ways.

For instance, the popularity of Vietnamese cuisine is evident in the rapid growth of Vietnamese restaurants in the United States as well as Canada. Specialty food stores in Vietnamese neighborhoods attract Vietnamese and non-Vietnamese customers alike.

One of the most popular Vietnamese dishes is *pho* (pronounced "fuh," a spicy chicken, beef, or pork broth served with rice noodles, fresh greens, bean sprouts, and a spicy sauce), which is eaten with chopsticks and a spoon. Like many other traditional Vietnamese dishes, *pho* is commonly seasoned with *nuoc mam*, a sauce made from a fermented mixture of fish, water, and sugar. This spicy blend also accompanies other typical dishes, such as *chao* (a rice porridge served with small pieces of chicken or beef, and lemon grass) and *cha gio* (an egg roll made of a seasoned mixture of eggs and ground pork rolled tightly in rice paper and deep-fried).

Vietnamese Americans have brought more than cuisine to their new homeland. Vietnamese music, both modern and traditional, is also making its mark in American society. Many mainstream record stores carry classical Vietnamese music that is popular among diverse audiences. The musical *Miss Saigon*, which tells the story of the last days of American involvement in Vietnam, enjoyed a long run on Broadway and is now performed in cities across the country.

In the entertainment industry, many Vietnamese Americans have gained recognition. In 1999 brothers and co-directors Timothy Linh Bui and Tony Bui won several Sundance Film Festival awards for their film *Three Seasons*. The movie was the first American production ever filmed in Vietnam, and the first U.S. film in which the actors spoke only Vietnamese. The brothers' next production, *The Green Dragon* (2002), features Vietnamese and English dialogue and tells the story of Vietnamese refugees newly arrived in the United States. Other Vietnamese Americans who have found success in the entertainment world include fashion supermodel Navia Nguyen and actors Kieu Chinh and Dustin Nguyen.

A large American audience is also enjoying Vietnamese literature. Vietnamese poetry is now being translated, published, and sold in bookstores. An expanding body of writing by immigrants has made accounts of often-harrowing escapes from Vietnam available to the American public. Meanwhile traditional Vietnamese folktales are making their way into bookstores and libraries. Tales about Vietnamese dragons, fairies, mythical tigers, and other folk themes include *The Golden Slipper* (a Vietnamese Cinderella tale), *Why the Rooster*

Crows at Sunrise, and *In the Land of the Small Dragon.*

Many Vietnamese have overcome great adversity to achieve the highest honors. They are valedictorians and salutatorians, top graduates of military academies, doctors, engineers, and successful businesspeople. In 2000 a nonprofit organization published *25 Vietnamese Americans in 25 Years.* The book celebrates Vietnamese American leaders and their impact on America over the past quarter-century. Honorees include the first Vietnamese American city council member, an NFL player, an astronaut, a MacArthur Fellowship recipient, journalists, filmmakers, community activists, and professors—all pioneers whose achievements exemplify what Vietnamese Americans have contributed to American society.

Economic Rebirth

In many cases, the arrival of Vietnamese immigrants in the cities has brought about positive change. Rundown neighborhoods have become vibrant, economically strong communities. In Orange County, California, for example, Vietnamese immigrants and refugees transformed vacant lots and boarded-up storefronts into a thriving city of busy restaurants, shops, and temples.

A Vietnamese dish of squid salad with dipping sauce. Increased Vietnamese immigration has helped generate an appreciation for Vietnamese cuisine by people of all ethnicities.

Legal Definition of a Refugee

Section 101(a)(42) of the U.S. Immigration and Nationality Act, as amended by the Refugee Relief Act of 1980, defines the term *refugee* in the following manner:

(A) Any person who is outside any country of such person's nationality or, in the case of a person having no nationality, is outside any country in which such person last habitually resided, and who is unable or unwilling to return to, and is unable or unwilling to avail himself or herself of protection of, that country because of persecution or a well-grounded fear of persecution on account of race, religion, nationality, membership in a particular social group, or political opinion, or

(B) In such special circumstances as the President, after appropriate consultation may specify, any person who is within the country of such person's nationality or, in the case of the person having no nationality, within the country in which such person is habitually residing, and who is persecuted or has a well-founded fear of persecution, on account of race, religion, nationality, membership in a particular social group, or political opinion. The term "refugee" does not include any person who ordered, incited, assisted, or otherwise participated in the persecution of any person on account of race, religion, nationality, membership in a particular social group, or political opinion.

Source: Immigration and Nationality Act, Section 101 Definitions. Bureau of Citizenship and Immigration Services website (http://www.immigration.gov)

The Vietnamese tradition of hard work and patience made this success story and many others like it possible, and future triumphs likely. Although their new life in Western society differs in many ways from their old life in Vietnam, the Vietnamese continue to hold on to the values, such as family loyalty and commitment to education, that make success in their new homeland possible.

Refugees and Immigrants

Most of those who came to North America from Vietnam in the 1970s are defined as *refugees*, people who fled their country to protect themselves from the horrors of war or persecution by a hostile government. However, most of those who come now are technically *immigrants*, people who willingly leave their country in search of prosperity and certain basic freedoms.

Few people expected that the rate of migration from Vietnam that existed in 1975 would remain high for long. Yet, for more than a quarter of a century, there has been a continuous flow of Vietnamese immigrants to North America. In 2001, more than 35,000 Vietnamese immigrated to the United States, according to the Bureau of Citizenship and Immigration Services (formerly the immigration services division of the Immigration and Naturalization Service). In 2002, 32,425 immigrants from Vietnam were admitted. That year Vietnam was one the greatest sources of immigrants to the United States, behind only Mexico, India, the People's Republic of China, and the Philippines. And there are no indications that the rate of Vietnamese migration to North America will decrease any time soon.

In the years since the Vietnam War (1957–75), a continuous flow of Vietnamese people has entered the United States and Canada. The majority of early immigrants were refugees escaping persecution; in more recent years they have been economic migrants.

2 REFUGEES FROM WAR

Officially known as the Socialist Republic of Vietnam, the country of Vietnam is located on the southeastern coast of Asia. It borders China to the north, Laos and Cambodia to the west, and the South China Sea to the south and east. The capital city of Hanoi is located in the northern part of Vietnam, while the country's largest urban center, Ho Chi Minh City (formerly Saigon), is located in the south.

A long and narrow country, Vietnam is a land of mountains, plains, and river deltas (swampy, triangular-shaped regions that sometimes form where rivers empty into seas). Northern Vietnam features jungle-covered mountains in the west and plains along the eastern seacoast. The Red River, a major tributary, forms a fertile delta where the Vietnamese have built dikes and canals to irrigate crops and control flooding. In the central region of Vietnam, the narrowest part of the country, mountains and highlands extend to the coast, occasionally dropping sharply to a narrow coastal plain. The country widens again in southern Vietnam, where the broad, fertile Mekong River Delta crosses low-lying plains. Like the Red River Delta to the north, much of the Mekong Delta is used for farming, especially Vietnam's principal crop of rice.

For thousands of years the majority of ethnic Vietnamese were agricultural people, mostly living in small villages in the two major delta regions and along the coast, where they grew rice in the wetlands. Other ethnic minorities lived by hunting

◀ A U.S. Army helicopter flies over villagers during the Vietnam War. The war, waged between North Vietnam and U.S.–backed South Vietnam, ended with the fall of the South Vietnamese capital of Saigon in 1975. Following the war, a refugee crisis left hundreds of thousands looking to resettle in another country.

and fishing in the central and northern mountains and highlands. From the 1950s to the 1970s, however, their peaceful way of life was severely disrupted, first by a war with the French, then by a civil war involving the United States. The Vietnam War (1957–75), which the Vietnamese refer to as "the American War," touched off large-scale emigration from Vietnam that continues today.

The Vietnam War

The roots of the Vietnam War stretch back to the late 1940s, just after the end of World War II (1939–45). Since the 1880s, the French had ruled Vietnam and the adjacent countries of Laos and Cambodia as a colony called Indochina. The European influence was so great in Vietnam that the country's major city of Saigon was known as "the Paris of the Orient."

During World War II, the Japanese occupied the Indochina region. Then, after the war ended, France reestablished its colonial government in the south. In northern Vietnam, however, a communist leader named Ho Chi Minh took control.

Determined that the Vietnamese had the right to rule themselves, General Ho established a government in the north called the Democratic Republic of Vietnam (DRVN). His forces, known as the

Ho Chi Minh was leader of the Democratic Republic of Vietnam (DRVN), or North Vietnam, and headed the military campaign to take control over South Vietnam until his death in 1969. After Saigon fell, the former capital was renamed Ho Chi Minh City.

Leaving Vietnam

In *Changing Identities: Vietnamese Americans, 1975–1995*, author James M. Freeman tells the story of Le Van Hieu, who was 13 years old when he and his family fled Vietnam:

> On the night of April 29, 1975, my life in Vietnam ended. I escaped in a small tugboat containing 55 people, 37 of whom were relatives, including my parents, my younger sister, and my three younger brothers.
>
> My father's younger brother, who was in the South Vietnamese navy, had outfitted the boat with food, water, and weapons. My father did not want to leave, even though he had spent four years in the USA and had been in the army and the government of South Vietnam. He only did so because his parents refused to leave unless he went with them.
>
> At first, I didn't think much about leaving. Then, around 11 a.m. the next morning, we heard over the radio that South Vietnam had fallen to the Communists. Then I realized I was not going to return. A sad feeling sank in. I felt empty.

Vietminh, began fighting a guerrilla war against the French. Eight years later, after suffering a major defeat at the battle of Dien Bien Phu, the French agreed to negotiate their withdrawal from Vietnam.

Representatives from France and the Democratic Republic of Vietnam met at a treaty conference in Geneva, Switzerland, in May 1954. The meeting was also attended by the United States, the United Kingdom, China, and the Soviet Union, whose governments were interested in the future of the region.

Ultimately, a decision was made to temporarily divide Vietnam in half, along the 17-degree northern latitude, also called the 17th parallel. According to the agreement, known as the Geneva Accords, France would withdraw all troops from areas north of this dividing line, while the communists agreed to vacate the south. In the north, Ho Chi Minh ruled the Democratic Republic of Vietnam, while in the south, Premier Ngo Dinh Diem led the Republic of Vietnam (RVN).

The agreement called for national elections in a reunited

country to be held in 1956. However, hostilities between North and South Vietnam quickly resumed, and the elections were never held. In 1957 a South Vietnamese rebel group tried to overthrow Diem's government, whose leaders were considered by some to be incompetent and corrupt. The group soon found support from the Viet Cong, a special military force loyal to Ho Chi Minh, who hoped to reunite the two countries under Ho's rule. The North Vietnamese government found support from two other communist countries—China and the Soviet Union.

Smoke rises from firebombed buildings in Saigon after the Viet Cong, a South Vietnamese military force loyal to Ho Chi Minh, launched the Tet Offensive, January 1968.

Meanwhile, the U.S. government, fearing the spread of communism in Southeast Asia, backed the South Vietnamese government. At first, the United States had only limited involvement in the war. It provided some military supplies and a few hundred advisors—soldiers who helped train the South Vietnamese army (ARVN). Over the years, however, South Vietnam needed more and more support, and the United States continued to send additional troops. By 1965, more than 500,000 Americans were fighting the war in Vietnam.

General Ho's guerrilla fighters proved effective. The war became increasingly unpopular back in the United States as thousands of American troops lost their lives. Soon U.S. citizens were protesting America's involvement in the Southeast Asian war and pressuring the government to withdraw its troops.

In January 1968, during a period of truce the Viet Cong made a surprise attack that became known as the Tet Offensive. Although the operation resulted in heavy losses for the Viet Cong, it demonstrated that the North Vietnamese could attack in urban areas, including the South Vietnamese capital of Saigon, and inflict damage. In *Vietnam: A History*, author Stanley Karnow explains how the impact of the offensive was political: "The Tet Offensive stunned President Johnson. Having swallowed most of the reports claiming that the Communists had been defanged, he had never imagined that they could attack the U.S. embassy in Saigon or assault the cities of South Vietnam." Less than two months later, with the war growing increasingly unpopular in America, Lyndon Johnson announced he would not seek re-election as president.

Nonetheless, five more years passed before the United States began to pull out of Vietnam. In 1973, President Richard Nixon signed a cease-fire agreement, along with the governments of North and South Vietnam. That year the first of the U.S. forces began to withdraw.

However, despite the South Vietnamese troops' low morale, lack of supplies, and reduced numbers, they continued to fight.

The war finally ended on April 30, 1975, when North Vietnamese forces overwhelmed South Vietnam's capital city of Saigon and the last of the U.S. troops frantically left the area. With the fall of the city, the South Vietnamese army pulled out, and the North Vietnamese army took control of the entire country.

The First Wave of Refugees (1975)

During the course of the war, only a relatively small number of refugees fled from Vietnam. But after Saigon fell, that small stream of refugees became a torrent. In the weeks that followed, approximately 135,000 Vietnamese soldiers, former government officials, and citizens fled the country. Most left in

A Prayer for Safe Shore

The foam of the ocean surrounds everything.
We are lost in the open sea, looking for a
shoreline to call safety.

We float on the deep and dark ocean
like dust on a palm leaf; we wander in endless space.
Our only fear, that we do not
sleep forever on the bottom of the sea.
We are without food or water and our children and women
lie exhausted, crying, until they can cry no more.

No ship will stop. We float like we do not exist.
Lord Buddha, do you hear our voices? From every
port we are pushed out. Our distress signals rise
and rise again.

How many boats have perished? How many families are buried
beneath those waves? Find us. We are lost in an open sea,
looking for a shoreline to call safety.

—Vietnamese monk, Los Angeles (translated from Vietnamese)

Source: Tenhula, John. *Voices from Southeast Asia: The Refugee Experience in the United States* (Ellis Island Series).

Escaping the destruction of the Tet Offensive, a group of young and old South Vietnamese continues its flight after crossing the Perfume River.

fear for their lives. Because they had worked against the will of the North Vietnamese government, they knew they would be prime targets for punishment, and possibly execution, at the hands of the advancing troops. With their families in tow, many South Vietnamese fled by whatever means possible.

Several thousand refugees, many of whom had worked with the American military or government, received U.S. assistance. They and their families managed to evacuate from the country during the same time the remaining American diplomats and troops were leaving. These refugees found passage on U.S. Navy ships or other military aircraft.

However, most other Vietnamese refugees had to make their own plans. Many escaped by sea on small boats. Others fled on foot, bringing along as many of their possessions as they could carry. Approximately one million civilians walked out of the city of Saigon, forming columns 20 miles (32 kilometers) long.

Aftermath of War

In 1976, a year after gaining control of South Vietnam, the communist regime unified the northern and southern regions into a single nation called the Socialist Republic of Vietnam. The country had suffered serious damage from the decades of bloody fighting. The once-lush green countryside was scarred and covered with land mines; chemical sprays had stripped foliage and vegetation and made sections of the land barren. Bombs had destroyed infrastructure that had delivered electricity, clean drinking water, and sanitary sewage disposal to the population.

War had also disrupted the traditional Vietnamese family structure. Millions of husbands and fathers had left their villages to join the fighting, leaving their families behind. In the years of warfare, nearly 2 million soldiers—from both the North and the South—had been killed, as well as more than 2 million citizens and approximately 57,000 American soldiers.

A young Vietnamese girl holding an infant child stands among the ruins of her bombed home, 1968. The losses in the Tet Offensive were a major setback for U.S. forces and the people of South Vietnam, who had to endure seven more years of fighting.

Vietnam's economy had also been devastated. The new government attempted to address this problem by instituting a program that called for the massive resettlement of Vietnamese citizens. Large numbers of city dwellers were forced to move to "New Economic Zones"—areas newly created for agricultural use. These state-run farms reflected the government's efforts to create a communist-model economy, but the resettlement program caused great hardships for urban people unused to farm labor, and the government threat of force would prove how such a system is nearly always inefficient.

An even harsher program forced thousands of former soldiers, policemen, or workers for the South Vietnamese or U.S. governments into "reeducation camps." These detainees, left behind during the chaotic evacuation in April 1975, were considered foes of the communist government. They were imprisoned in camps in the north, where they were subjected to indoctrination, hard physical labor, and torture. Some died, and others were detained for up to 15 years.

The communist government's resettlement program did not resolve the economic crisis in Vietnam, and even made the situation worse for many people. There were families reduced to extreme poverty, who managed to survive only by pooling their meager resources with other members of their extended families. Oppressed by the communist government, many Vietnamese feared and distrusted each other. They worried that if they said or did the wrong thing, neighborhood spies would turn them over to the government for punishment. Under the increasingly oppressive communist rule, many Vietnamese citizens lost their freedoms, and some even their lives.

Despite its reunification, Vietnam did not find peace. Two more military conflicts further harmed the country's weak economy and shattered the morale of its people. In 1978 the Socialist Republic of Vietnam invaded Cambodia in a war that would not officially end until 1991. In 1979, in retaliation for the incursion into Cambodia, China took over Vietnam's northern border for about a month.

The Second and Third Waves (1977–83)

During the late 1970s, as conditions in unified Vietnam worsened, a second wave of more than 125,000 refugees fled the country. Most of the refugees in this group were ethnic Chinese Vietnamese—traditionally the merchant class in Vietnam—who were being forced out of the country by the Vietnamese government. Other ethnic groups, whose members had served as educators or in the South Vietnamese military or government, also fled out of fear of persecution during this time.

Soon afterward, a third wave of refugees began to leave. Most of these refugees were Vietnamese fisherman and farmers, who fled along with their families. About 20,000 sought to escape from the country, fleeing by foot to Cambodia. Hundreds of thousands more tried to leave in boats, which in most cases were poorly made and overcrowded to the point of sinking. These refugees, who came to be known as "the boat people," straggled in tiny boats across the Gulf of Thailand or the South China Sea, although many lacked experience with sea travel and navigation. Countless numbers of these refugees died, victims of brutal pirate attacks or drowning. Survivors searched for sanctuary in neighboring countries, most often the closest nations of Thailand and Malaysia. Some traveled as far as the shores of South Korea and Japan.

But Thailand and Malaysia, and other nearby nations such as Hong Kong, Indonesia, and the Philippines, did not have the means to support the deluge of refugees attempting to reach their shores. The first waves of boat people were often turned away, by local inhabitants as well as by government naval ships.

A Desperate Journey

Most Vietnamese refugees left in a great hurry, intent on getting out of the country as quickly as possible in order to save their lives. With simply no time to make plans, they gave little consideration to their ultimate destination, focusing mostly on escaping the country. As a result, during the journey out of Vietnam many refugees suffered from cold, thirst, and hunger because of inadequate supplies, or they became lost because they had no guide or map to follow.

Refugees traveling by foot walked with the fear of stepping on land mines or unexploded ordnance. They agonized about meeting up with roving bands of robbers or North Vietnamese forces, who were known to shell refugees as they fled to Cambodia. The journey by sea was just as perilous as Thai pirates overtook boats loaded with refugees and overcrowded vessels sank.

In his book *The Vietnamese Experience in America*, author Paul James Rutledge described the refugee experience of a Vietnamese woman named Soon. Born in South Vietnam, near the town of Bien Hoa, Soon had grown up during the war. When the U.S. military forces first entered the country, her two older sons had joined the South Vietnamese army in the fight against the North Vietnamese. After the fall of Saigon, Soon knew that she and her family were in danger. The seven remaining family members, including Soon, her three daughters and youngest son, her grandson, and her daughter-in-law, stole

Dozens of Vietnamese refugees, nicknamed "boat people," rest in a temporary camp in the Hong Kong Government dock-yard, 1979. Several waves of refugees followed the first major refugee crisis of 1975.

away from their village in the middle of the night, ever fearful of being turned in by communist spies.

The family members traveled on foot, at first heading for Cambodia, where they hoped to find shelter and make further arrangements. However, the journey proved harder than they expected. They were encouraged by the reports that boats along the shore of the South China Sea were taking Vietnamese to American ships, which were then taking people to the United States.

After weeks of traveling by foot, with the constant fear of losing food and money to pickpockets and bandits, the family decided that leaving Vietnam by boat would be a better option. When they reached the harbor, however, Soon and her family found bedlam there. Hundreds of frightened refugees were also trying to leave the country. They were bartering frantically with the owners of fishing boats, offering food, possessions, and other valuables for the privilege of passage to safety.

The family managed to obtain a place on an overcrowded

Carrying pots and other belongings, Vietnamese refugees travel in search of safety. The refugee journey to a safe destination often has entailed great dangers over land and on the seas, where boat people are vulnerable to harsh weather and pirating.

boat. But it never met up with the American ship that they were promised. After three days, the vessel was adrift at sea, with its captain completely disoriented. In two horrifying instances, Thai pirates descended on the group, stealing money and personal belongings, killing passengers, and kidnapping several young girls and boys. Finally, after six days at sea, the remaining refugees spotted the Malaysian coast. In their haste to reach land, a number of passengers jumped overboard and tried to swim to shore. In the struggle to reach the beach, some were swamped by waves and drowned.

Once on shore, the refugees were driven back by an angry group of Malaysians wielding knives and throwing rocks. In despair the refugees staggered back into the water. Some were swept to their deaths by the ocean currents as they tried to return to the boat. The remaining Vietnamese, confused and frightened, continued to drift along the coast in search of a safe place to land. They were terrorized several more times by local inhabitants, who refused to allow them to land, before they finally were rescued by Malaysian government officials. Soon and her family were among the few who survived the arduous journey from their homeland to a Malaysian refugee camp. She then stayed in several refugee camps before making her way to the United States in 1979, and eventually settling in central Oklahoma.

Countries of Asylum

Boat people who survived their perilous journeys often ended up in hastily prepared camps that were established in the countries of first asylum—Thailand, Malaysia, or the Philippines. The Vietnamese had to remain in these countries of first asylum until more permanent resettlement arrangements could be made. Some were eventually moved to countries of second asylum, such as Hong Kong, Indonesia, Singapore, or Japan, where they lived in what were supposed to be temporary camps. After months and even years of waiting for word that a host country would accept them, successful applicants were dispersed to countries all over the world, including the United States, Canada, Australia, China, and France. Others would spend years at the camps, waiting for news that they a country would accept them.

The Southeast Asian countries surrounding Vietnam were poorly prepared for the sudden influx of refugees. Few had economies strong enough to handle the needy people, so most of the refugee camps were undersupplied. International agencies such as the United Nations High Commissioner for Refugees (UNHCR), the Red Cross of Thailand, the Red Crescent of Malaysia, and organizations from Canada, Australia, and the United States provided various kinds of assistance. However, most camp facilities lacked sufficient food, water, and medical services.

An example of a typical refugee camp was Pilau Bidong, named after the Malaysian island where it was established. Located 18 miles (29 km) off the coast of Malaysia, the island of Pilau Bidong was uninhabited in July 1978. Just five months later it was home to 25,000 Vietnamese. Like most Vietnamese refugee camps, Pilau Bidong was severely overcrowded and lacked even the basic necessities to build temporary shelters. Refugees dealt with contaminated well water, medicine shortages, and inadequate food rations (a half pint of rice per day and a tin of sardines every five days).

Camp residents tried to make the best of the situation by organizing to improve their living conditions. Individuals were placed in charge of specific needs, such as supplies, security, construction, health, water supply, sanitation, and interpreters. Despite these efforts, life at Pilau Bidong continued to become harsher as the population grew to about 42,000. Residents lived in makeshift houses, some three stories high, constructed of timber beams, cardboard or tin walls, and roofs of plastic sheeting. Rotting rubbish and human excrement fouled the beaches of the tiny island, creating an overwhelming stench in the heat. Wells had dried up or become polluted, causing severe water shortages. For many Vietnamese, the desperate journey out of Vietnam had brought them into a desperate living environment—one in which some refugees would remain stuck many years.

Vietnam's Struggling Economy

Vietnam had not been a wealthy nation before the war, and after the communists took over the country, it dropped to the bottom of Asia's economic ladder. The programs instituted by the new regime during the mid-1970s caused Vietnam's economy to lag further behind those of other Southeast Asian countries.

Communism is a system in which the state owns nearly all property and controls most of the industry. In 1976 the Vietnamese government, which already managed agricultural and industrial enterprises in the north, took over the privately owned business and farming operations in the south. However, government control resulted in lowered production, and Vietnam's economy weakened to the point that the country became one of the poorest in the world. A U.S. trade embargo, imposed on Vietnam at the end of the war, pushed the country further into decline.

Ten years later, the Vietnamese government recognized the need for change. In the mid-1980s, it introduced a series of new economic reforms called *doi moi*, or "renewal." Instead of government involvement in all aspects of the economy, *doi moi* allowed for some types of private enterprise and competition. The reforms were the first steps away from a government-run economy toward a market-oriented one.

Still, despite the advances toward economic reform, the country continued to have a high poverty rate. And ongoing political oppression by the communist government continued to drive many Vietnamese from their homeland during the 1980s and 1990s.

3 A Continuing Exodus

Years after the fall of Saigon, the rate of refugees attempting to leave Southeast Asia remained steady. Many Vietnamese hoped to eventually resettle in the United States, which was accepting hundreds of thousands of immigrants. This willingness to accept immigrants from Asia had not always been characteristic of the United States, which has had a changing immigration policy throughout its history.

A Short History of U.S. Immigration

Immigration to the United States has been characterized by openness punctuated by periods of restriction. During the 17th, 18th, and 19th centuries, immigration was essentially open without restriction, and, at times, immigrants were even recruited to come to America. Between 1783 and 1820, approximately 250,000 immigrants arrived at U.S. shores. Between 1841 and 1860, more than 4 million immigrants came; most were from England, Ireland, and Germany.

Historically, race and ethnicity have played a role in legislation to restrict immigration. The Chinese Exclusion Act of 1882, which was not repealed until 1943, specifically prevented Chinese people from becoming U.S. citizens and did not allow Chinese laborers to immigrate for the next decade. An agreement with Japan in the early 1900s prevented most Japanese immigration to the United States.

Until the 1920s, no numerical restrictions on immigration

◀During the early years of immigration, Asian immigrants were processed through this station on Angel Island, located in the San Francisco Bay. The station, nicknamed the "Ellis Island of the West," was first put into operation in 1910.

existed in the United States, although health restrictions applied. The only other significant restrictions came in 1917, when passing a literacy test became a requirement for immigrants. Presidents Cleveland, Taft, and Wilson had vetoed similar measures earlier. In addition, in 1917 a prohibition was added to the law against the immigration of people from Asia (defined as the Asiatic barred zone). While a few of these prohibitions were lifted during World War II, they were not repealed until 1952, and even then Asians were only allowed in under very small annual quotas.

Immigration Policy After World War I

During World War I, the federal government required that all travelers to the United States obtain a visa at a U.S. consulate or diplomatic post abroad. As former State Department consular affairs officer C. D. Scully points out, by making that requirement permanent Congress, by 1924, established the framework of temporary, or non-immigrant visas (for study, work, or travel), and immigrant visas (for permanent residence). That framework remains in place today.

After World War I, cultural intolerance and bizarre racial theories led to new immigration restrictions. The House Judiciary Committee employed a eugenics consultant, Dr. Harry N. Laughlin, who asserted that certain races were inferior. Another leader of the eugenics movement, Madison Grant, argued that Jews, Italians, and others were inferior because of their supposedly different skull size.

The Immigration Act of 1924, preceded by the Temporary Quota Act of 1921, set new numerical limits on immigration based on "national origin." Taking effect in 1929, the 1924 act set annual quotas on immigrants that were specifically designed to keep out southern Europeans, such as Italians and Greeks. Generally no more than 100 people of the proscribed nationalities were permitted to immigrate.

While the new law was rigid, the U.S. Department of State's restrictive interpretation directed consular officers overseas to be even stricter in their application of the "public charge" provision. (A public charge is someone unable to support himself or his family.) As author Laura Fermi wrote, "In response to the new cry for restriction at the beginning of the [Great Depression] . . . the consuls were to interpret very strictly the clause prohibiting admission of aliens 'likely to become public charges; and to deny the visa to an applicant who in their opinion might become a public charge at any time.'"

In the early 1900s, more than one million immigrants a year came to the United States. In 1930—the first year of the national-origin quotas—approximately 241,700 immigrants were admitted. But under the State Department's strict interpretations, only 23,068 immigrants entered during 1933, the smallest total since 1831. Later these restrictions prevented many Jews in Germany and elsewhere in Europe from escaping what would become the Holocaust. At the height of the Holocaust in 1943, the United States admitted fewer than 6,000 refugees.

The Displaced Persons Act of 1948, the nation's first refugee law, allowed many refugees from World War II to settle in the United States. The law put into place policy changes that had already seen immigration rise from 38,119 in 1945 to 108,721 in 1946 (and later to 249,187 in 1950). One-third of those admitted between 1948 and 1951 were Poles, with ethnic Germans forming the second-largest group.

The 1952 Immigration and Nationality Act is best known for its restrictions against those who supported communism or anarchy. However, the bill's other provisions were quite restrictive and were passed over the veto of President Truman. The 1952 act retained the national-origin quota system for the Eastern Hemisphere. The Western Hemisphere continued to operate without a quota and relied on other qualitative factors to limit immigration. Moreover, during that time, the Mexican bracero program, from 1942 to 1964, allowed millions of Mexican agricultural workers to work temporarily in the United States.

The 1952 act set aside half of each national quota to be divided among three preference categories for relatives of U.S. citizens and permanent residents. The other half went to aliens with high education or exceptional abilities. These quotas applied only to those from the Eastern Hemisphere.

A Halt to the National-Origin Quotas

The Immigration and Nationality Act of 1965 became a landmark in immigration legislation by specifically striking the racially based national-origin quotas. It removed the barriers to Asian immigration, which later led to opportunities to immigrate for many Filipinos, Chinese, Koreans, and others. The Western Hemisphere was designated a ceiling of 120,000 immigrants but without a preference system or per country limits. Modifications made in 1978 ultimately combined the Western and Eastern Hemispheres into one preference system and one ceiling of 290,000.

In 1965 President Lyndon Johnson signed the Immigration and Nationality Act, which inaugurated a new era of immigration. Thousands of Asians and other foreign groups were able to immigrate to the United States after the act was passed.

The 1965 act built on the existing system—without the national-origin quotas—and gave somewhat more priority to family relationships. It did not completely overturn the existing system but rather carried forward essentially intact the family immigration categories from the 1959 amendments to the Immigration and Nationality Act. Even though the text of the law prior to 1965 indicated that half of the immigration slots were reserved for skilled employment immigration, in practice, Immigration and Naturalization Service (INS) statistics show that 86 percent of the visas issued between 1952 and 1965 went for family immigration.

A number of significant pieces of legislation since 1980 have shaped the current U.S. immigration system. First, the Refugee Act of 1980 removed refugees from the annual world limit and established that the president would set the number of refugees who could be admitted each year after consultations with Congress.

Second, the 1986 Immigration Reform and Control Act (IRCA) introduced sanctions against employers who "knowingly" hired undocumented immigrants (those here illegally). It also provided amnesty for many undocumented immigrants.

Third, the Immigration Act of 1990 increased legal immigration by 40 percent. In particular, the act significantly increased the number of employment-based immigrants (to 140,000), while also boosting family immigration.

Fourth, the 1996 Illegal Immigration Reform and Immigrant Responsibility Act (IIRAIRA) significantly tightened rules that permitted undocumented immigrants to convert to legal status and made other changes that tightened immigration law in areas such as political asylum and deportation.

Fifth, in response to the September 11, 2001, terrorist attacks, the USA PATRIOT Act and the Enhanced Border Security and Visa Entry Reform Act tightened rules on the granting of visas to individuals from certain countries and enhanced the federal government's monitoring and detention authority over foreign nationals in the United States.

New U.S. Immigration Agencies

In a dramatic reorganization of the federal government, the Homeland Security Act of 2002 abolished the Immigration and Naturalization Service and transferred its immigration service and enforcement functions from the Department of Justice into a new Department of Homeland Security. The Customs Service, the Coast Guard, and parts of other agencies were also transferred into the new department.

The Department of Homeland Security, with regards to immigration, is organized as follows: The Bureau of Customs and Border Protection (BCBP) contains Customs and Immigration

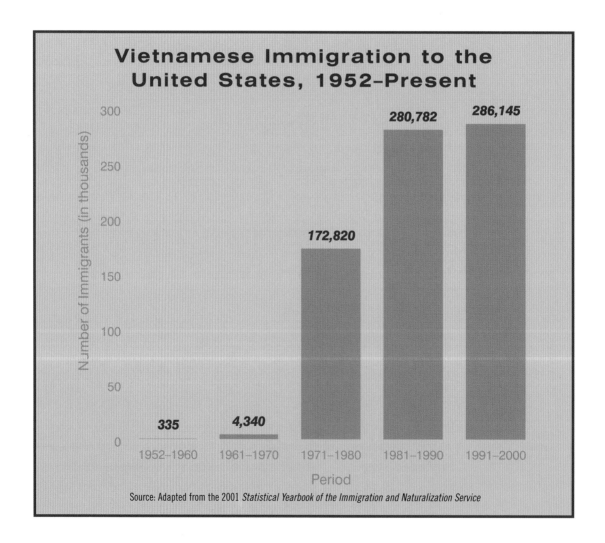

Vietnamese Immigration to the United States, 1952–Present

Source: Adapted from the 2001 *Statistical Yearbook of the Immigration and Naturalization Service*

President Bush signs the Enhanced Border Security and Visa Entry Reform Act with congressional members in attendance, May 2002. The act, along with the USA PATRIOT Act, was passed in response to the September 2001 terrorist attacks.

inspectors, who check the documents of travelers to the United States at air, sea, and land ports of entry; and Border Patrol agents, the uniformed agents who seek to prevent unlawful entry along the southern and northern border. The new Bureau of Immigration and Customs Enforcement (BICE) employs investigators, who attempt to find undocumented immigrants inside the United States, and Detention and Removal officers, who detain and seek to deport such individuals. The new Bureau of Citizenship and Immigration Services (BCIS) is where people go, or correspond with, to become U.S. citizens or obtain permission to work or extend their stay in the United States.

Following the terrorist attacks of September 11, 2001, the Department of Justice adopted several measures that did not require new legislation to be passed by Congress. Some of these measures created controversy and raised concerns about civil liberties. For example, FBI and INS agents detained for months more than 1,000 foreign nationals of Middle Eastern descent and refused to release the names of the individuals. It is alleged that the Department of Justice adopted tactics that discouraged the detainees from obtaining legal assistance. The Department of Justice also began requiring foreign nationals from primarily Muslim nations to be fingerprinted and questioned by immigration officers upon entry or if they have been living in the United States. Those involved in the September 11 attacks were not immigrants—people who become permanent residents with a right to stay in the United States—but holders of temporary visas, primarily visitor or tourist visas.

Immigration to the United States Today

Today, the annual rate of legal immigration is lower than that at earlier periods in U.S. history. For example, from 1901 to 1910 approximately 10.4 immigrants per 1,000 U.S. residents came to the United States. Today, the annual rate is about 3.5 immigrants per 1,000 U.S. residents. While the percentage of foreign-born people in the U.S. population has risen above 11 percent, it remains lower than the 13 percent or higher that prevailed in the country from 1860 to 1930. Still, as has been the case previously in U.S. history, some people argue that even legal immigration should be lowered. These people maintain that immigrants take jobs native-born Americans could fill and that U.S. population growth, which immigration contributes to, harms the environment. In 1996 Congress voted against efforts to reduce legal immigration.

Most immigrants (800,000 to one million annually) enter the United States legally. But over the years the undocumented (illegal) portion of the population has increased to about 2.8 percent of the U.S. population—approximately 8 million people in all.

Today, the legal immigration system in the United States contains many rules, permitting only individuals who fit into certain categories to immigrate—and in many cases only after waiting anywhere from 1 to 10 years or more, depending on the demand in that category. The system, representing a compromise among family, employment, and human rights concerns, has the following elements:

A U.S. citizen may sponsor for immigration a spouse, parent, sibling, or minor or adult child.

A lawful permanent resident (green card holder) may sponsor only a spouse or child.

A foreign national may immigrate if he or she gains an employer sponsor.

An individual who can show that he or she has a "well-founded fear of persecution" may come to the country as a refugee—or be allowed to stay as an asylee (someone who receives asylum).

Beyond these categories, essentially the only other way to immigrate is to apply for and receive one of the "diversity" visas, which are granted annually by lottery to those from "underrepresented" countries.

In 1996 changes to the law prohibited nearly all incoming

A mother and her children prepare to evacuate Saigon following the city's fall to the North Vietnamese, April 1975. Beginning in 1976, many Vietnamese could resettle in the United States, although in many cases the journey from Vietnam was dangerous.

immigrants from being eligible for federal public benefits, such as welfare, during their first five years in the country. Refugees were mostly excluded from these changes. In addition, families who sponsor relatives must sign an affidavit of support showing they can financially take care of an immigrant who falls on hard times.

Legislation and Programs Affecting Early Vietnamese Refugees

In the United States the first Refugee Relief Act (RRA), which became law in 1953, and its amendments allowed for the admission of people persecuted by communist governments. Because Vietnam had become a communist country in 1976, large numbers of Vietnamese refugees qualified for refugee status and could enter the United States for resettlement.

In response to the extensive loss of life among the boat people during the late 1970s, the United Nations High Commissioner for Refugees instituted a program that would allow for safer migration. The UN agency negotiated an agreement with the Vietnamese government that allowed persons accepted by another country to leave Vietnam under an Orderly Departure Program (ODP). Under the ODP, a person could enter a host country if he or she had close relatives living there who applied to bring them over. These relations could be spouses, sons, daughters, parents, grandparents, or unmarried grandchildren. People could also qualify if they were ethnic Vietnamese who had worked for the U.S. government in Vietnam for at least one year since 1962. A third way to receive permission under the ODP was if the person could show an established connection to the United States, whether as a student enrolled in a school there; as someone persecuted because of his or her association with the U.S. government or military; or as the child of a Vietnamese mother and American soldier (Amerasian).

Around the same time, the U.S. Congress passed the Refugee Act of 1980, which incorporated the United Nations' definition

A Long Wait

Although hundreds of thousands of Vietnamese eventually left Southeast Asian refugee camps for resettlement in the United States, Canada, and other nations, a significant number of other refugees stayed behind. Some remained in these camps for more than a decade, waiting fruitlessly for a host country to accept them. During the 1980s approximately 76,000 Vietnamese camp residents were moved back to Vietnam, with the assistance of the United Nations High Commissioner for Refugees. Vietnam had agreed to take them back with the understanding that they would not be punished for trying to escape.

In early 1995, another 37,000 refugees were still living in refugee camps based in the Philippines, Hong Kong, and Malaysia. Many local residents resented the camps, and they became targets for violence. A camp in the Philippines was attacked that year and burned down.

In 1996, all the camps in Asia were closed, and the Vietnamese residents were repatriated (sent back to their homeland). Altogether more than 112,000 boat people were sent back to Vietnam. However, they were returned with the promise that the U.S. government would interview them one more time once they were back in Vietnam. There they would be given a final opportunity to request permission to live in the United States, as long as they qualified under the legal definition of a refugee.

of a refugee as a person "unable or unwilling to return to or be put under the protection of the country in which they last habitually resided" because of "persecution or a well-founded fear of persecution on account of race, religion, nationality, membership in a particular social group, or political opinion." The act also standardized the process and services for admitting and resettling refugees within the country.

Applicants under the Orderly Departure Program were processed in Ho Chi Minh City and flown to host countries. The program enjoyed some success; however, during the mid-1980s, disputes arose between Vietnam and host countries over the eligibility requirements for Vietnamese trying to leave through the program. This significantly slowed the rate of departures for a few years, until 1987, when the program resumed normal operations.

The Fourth Wave of Migration (1983–89)

People coming into the United States under the ODP were processed either as refugees or as immigrants under the Immigrant and Nationality Act. The fourth wave of Vietnamese immigration, arriving between 1983 and 1989, included people seeking political asylum from the oppressive communist government.

After years of negotiations, the U.S. Department of State reached an agreement with the Vietnamese government in 1988 allowing for the release of detainees in reeducation camps. Many of these political prisoners were former high-ranking

Amerasian Homecoming Act

After the Vietnam War ended, many people were concerned about the children born to Vietnamese women and American soldiers. Called "Amerasian" because of their mixed American and Asian heritage, these children were shunned by Vietnamese society, and because their fathers were acknowledged enemies of the state, they were rejected by the communist government. They were not allowed to attend school or receive other public services.

It is not known how many Amerasian children, commonly referred to as *bui doi*, or "the dust of life," lived in Vietnam. The numbers range from 10,000 to more than 200,000.

Although the U.S. government offered to accept the Amerasians as refugees, the Vietnamese government refused to acknowledge that the children were persecuted (which would have made them eligible for refugee status). Finally, in December 1987, the U.S. Congress passed the Amerasian Homecoming Act, a law that allows Amerasians to be admitted to the United States as "immigrants." With this designation, they can leave under the Orderly Departure Program.

According to the act, an Amerasian is defined as a person born in Vietnam after January 1, 1962, and before January 1, 1976, who is fathered by a citizen of the United States. Those who qualify may bring a spouse, children, parent, or guardian along with them. In the late 1980s, about 39,000 Amerasian children were admitted to the United States under the Amerasian Homecoming Act. By the end of the 20th century, that number had grown to almost 90,000.

South Vietnamese government officials and military officers, who were now allowed to exit the country under the Orderly Departure Program. Political detainees who had been employed by Americans or American companies in Vietnam, or officials, soldiers, and their close relatives who had been associated with the United States, also qualified for the program.

Eventually an estimated 100,000 people, many newly released from reeducation camps or escapees, were allowed to join family members overseas. Altogether, about 400,000 people arrived in the U.S. via the Orderly Departure Program.

In addition, the U.S. Congress has passed laws that, at the present, require the State Department to continue processing and considering refugees' cases out of concern that individuals who may have been imprisoned by the communist government did not have every opportunity to pursue refugee status before. The State Department was also acting on concerns that the U.S. government had used Vietnamese government interpreters who may have made it difficult for a number of refugees to speak freely, or who may not have passed along all relevant information to U.S. officials.

Vietnam Today

More than 81 million people live in the Socialist Republic of Vietnam, giving the country the second-largest population in Southeast Asia, and the 13th largest in the world. Vietnam has an average of more than 525 people for every square mile, making it one of the world's most densely populated countries.

The government allows only one political party—the Vietnamese Communist Party. Restrictions on free speech, free press, freedom of assembly, and other civil liberties remain in place, and perceived opponents, such as political and religious dissidents, are jailed and punished.

With the economic changes brought about by *doi moi*, first instituted in 1986, the country has made significant improvements as its economy has opened up to more trade with the outside world, including South Korea and Japan. By the end of the 1990s the standard of living for some of the population had improved as Vietnam made significant progress in the fields of health care, art and culture, sports, and education. The average life expectancy of the Vietnamese people is about 70 years, which is high compared with that of similarly poor countries. Significant success in the field of education has produced a high literacy rate of almost 94 percent of Vietnamese over 15 years old.

However, the country cannot yet claim to have a healthy, market-oriented economy. The communist government remains unreceptive and sometimes hostile to the foreign investment required to develop such a system. Because of such policies, improvements in the nation's economic health have come slowly. Today more than a third of the Vietnamese population (37 percent) still lives below the poverty line. In 2001 the country's per capita gross domestic product, or GDP (the value of all

Vietnamese people ride their bicycles in a street of Saigon. Vietnam has one of the world's densest populations—there are an estimated 525 or more people for every square mile.

A group of young Vietnamese students sit in a classroom in the northern province of Thanh Hoa. The recent improvements in Vietnam's educational system have resulted in an impressive national literacy rate of 94 percent.

goods and services produced within a nation in a given year per person) was $2,100. This amount is significantly less than the per capita GDPs of the United States ($36,300 in 2001) or Canada ($29,400 in 2002).

Fifth Wave of Migration (1989–Present)

A fifth wave of immigration from Vietnam continues today. It includes the immigrants who left Vietnam after March 14, 1989. That date marked the beginning of an international agreement called the Comprehensive Plan of Action. Approved by the International Conference on Indochinese Refugees, held in Geneva, Switzerland, the Comprehensive Plan of Action allows Vietnamese seeking to leave the country to be screened for refugee status. Those who qualify are allowed to resettle in other countries, including the United States. Those who do not qualify remain in Vietnam. The plan also provides for the return to Vietnam of Asian refugee-camp residents who had been determined ineligible for refugee status.

Each year only about 2,000 Vietnamese come to the United States as designated refugees. Many are political detainees from the communist reeducation camps or the grown children of American soldiers. Hundreds of others qualify as refugees under the U.S. Resettlement Opportunities for Vietnamese Returnees program—they are from among the thousands repatriated from Asian refugee camps. The last of these camps closed in 1996, but refugees received a promise from the U.S. government that they would be rescreened. If they can prove "a well-grounded fear of persecution," they qualify as refugees and can resettle in the United States.

Today, the majority of Vietnamese leave as immigrants, including Amerasians and family members processed through "orderly departure" and ordinary immigration channels. From the 1990s to the early 2000s, the flow of Vietnamese migration to the United States remained high, averaging about 25,000 to 35,000 people per year. The majority of these immigrants were the relatives of those who arrived earlier—parents, children, spouses, or siblings who had been left behind.

A November 2000 story in the *New York Times* on Vietnamese immigration to the United States discussed the trend of family reunification in the U.S. In the article, 74-year-old Vietnam resident Nguyen Xuan Hien explained that his 11-year-old granddaughter was receiving the documentation to emigrate from Vietnam so that she could be reunited with her parents in New Orleans, Louisiana. "I would go too if I had the money," he added. "She'll have a better life there. Conditions here in Vietnam are not perfect, you know."

A Short History of Canadian Immigration

In the 1800s, immigration into Canada was largely unrestricted. Farmers and artisans from England and Ireland made up a significant portion of 19th-century immigrants. England's Parliament passed laws that facilitated and encouraged the voyage to North America, particularly for the poor.

After the United States barred Chinese railroad workers from settling in the country, Canada encouraged the immigration of Chinese laborers to assist in the building of Canadian railways. Responding to the racial views of the time, the Canadian Parliament began charging a "head tax" for Chinese and South Asian (Indian) immigrants in 1885. The fee of $50—later raised to $500—was well beyond the means of laborers making one or two dollars a day. Later, the government sought additional ways to prohibit Asians from entering the country. For example, it decided to require a "continuous journey," meaning that immigrants to Canada had to travel from their country on a boat that made an uninterrupted passage. For immigrants or asylum seekers from Asia this was nearly impossible.

As the 20th century progressed, concerns about race led to further restrictions on immigration to Canada. These restrictions

Lester Pearson, prime minister of Canada from 1963 to 1968, believed that immigrants were key to the country's economic growth. In 1966 the Canadian government introduced a policy statement stressing the importance of an open system of immigration.

particularly hurt Jewish and other refugees seeking to flee persecution in Europe. Government statistics indicate that Canada accepted no more than 5,000 Jewish refugees before and during the Holocaust.

After World War II, Canada, like the United States, began accepting thousands of Europeans displaced by the war. Canada's laws were modified to accept these war refugees, as well as Hungarians fleeing Communist authorities after the crushing of the 1956 Hungarian Revolution.

The Immigration Act of 1952 in Canada allowed for a "tap on, tap off" approach to immigration, granting administrative authorities the power to allow more immigrants into the country in good economic times, and fewer in times of recession. The shortcoming of such an approach is that there is little evidence immigrants harm a national economy and much evidence they contribute to economic growth, particularly in the growth of the labor force.

In 1966 the government of Prime Minister Lester Pearson introduced a policy statement stressing how immigrants were key to Canada's economic growth. With Canada's relatively small population base, it became clear that in the absence of newcomers, the country would not be able to grow. The policy was introduced four years after Parliament enacted important legislation that eliminated Canada's own version of racially based national-origin quotas.

In 1967 a new law established a points system that awarded entry to potential immigrants using criteria based primarily on an individual's age, language ability, skills, education, family relationships, and job prospects. The total points needed for entry of an immigrant is set by the Minister of Citizenship and Immigration Canada. The new law also established a category for humanitarian (refugee) entry.

The 1976 Immigration Act refined and expanded the possibility for entry under the points system, particularly for those seeking to sponsor family members. The act also expanded refugee and asylum law to comport with Canada's international obligations. The law established five basic categories for immigration into Canada: 1) family; 2) humanitarian; 3) independents (including skilled workers), who immigrate to Canada on their own; 4) assisted relatives; and 5) business immigrants (including investors, entrepreneurs, and the self-employed).

The new Immigration and Refugee Protection Act, which took effect June 28, 2002, made a series of modifications to existing Canadian immigration law. The act, and the regulations that followed, toughened rules on those seeking asylum and the process for removing people unlawfully in Canada.

The law modified the points system, adding greater flexibility for skilled immigrants and temporary workers to become permanent residents, and evaluating skilled workers on the weight of their transferable skills as well as those of their specific occupation. The legislation also made it easier for employers to have a labor shortage declared in an industry or sector, which would facilitate the entry of foreign workers in that industry or sector.

On family immigration, the act permitted parents to sponsor dependent children up to the age of 22 (previously 19 was the maximum age at which a child could be sponsored for immigration). The act also allowed partners in common-law arrangements, including same-sex partners, to be considered as family members for the purpose of immigration sponsorship. Along with these liberalizing measures, the act also included provisions to address perceived gaps in immigration-law enforcement.

Vietnamese Immigration to Canada

Like the United States, Canada contained very few people of Vietnamese descent during the 1950s and 1960s. At that time Vietnamese migrants consisted primarily of students enrolled at the universities in Quebec, Ottawa, and Moncton, New Brunswick, where their fluency in the French language (because of France's occupation of Vietnam) eased the transition to living abroad. After graduating, many Vietnamese students remained in Canada, so that by 1970 approximately 1,200

people of Vietnamese origin were living in the country.

A significant wave of migration—around 6,500 political refugees—started after the fall of the South Vietnamese government in 1975. Most of the refugees settled in the cities of Montreal, Toronto, Calgary, Edmonton, and Vancouver. By the end of 1978, the total Vietnamese population in Canada had reached 10,000.

Over the next two years, the Canadian government accepted almost 60,000 boat people from camps in Thailand, Malaysia, and Hong Kong. Many of these refugees were ethnic Vietnamese and Vietnamese Chinese. Because about 30,000 of them were resettled under the sponsorship of various private organizations and churches of Canada, they ended up living in regions throughout the country.

From 1981 to 1986, approximately 24,000 Vietnamese came to Canada as refugees, while another 17,000 were accepted as

Vancouver received a large segment of Vietnamese refugees settling in Canada during the first refugee crisis. Montreal, Toronto, Calgary, and Edmonton also opened their doors to many of these refugees.

immigrants. In the years that followed, immigration to Canada from Vietnam remained at a steady rate; newcomers typically were sponsored by relatives and family members, private groups, and the government. As of the turn of the 21st century, almost 150,000 people living in Canada claim Vietnamese descent.

4 LIFE IN A NEW HOMELAND

Since 1975 more than 2 million people have left Vietnam. Over half have settled in North America, where like all immigrants, they have encountered the challenges of finding their place in a new land.

The first wave of Vietnamese immigrants—those who left just after the fall of Saigon—differed from those who came later. For the most part, these earliest arrivals—numbering around 130,000—were well educated and could speak English. Among these earliest arrivals were high-ranking soldiers, professionals who had worked with American military personnel or American companies doing business in Vietnam, ethnic Vietnamese with a U.S. education, and individuals with family in the United States.

Because many in the first wave of Vietnamese refugees already had relatives in the United States, the U.S. government did not need to provide for their entry and survival in their new homeland. Many simply moved into established households. However, most were first brought to refugee camps established at U.S. military bases located in Thailand and the Philippines, then to bases on Wake Island, Subic Bay, or Guam, before being taken to the United States.

U.S. Refugee Camps

Shortly before the fall of Saigon the U.S. government set up temporary housing for Vietnamese refugees at four military

◀A young Vietnamese American couple stands in front of a shopping mall in Little Saigon, an Orange County community in the town of Westminster, just south of Los Angeles. Little Saigon is the largest Vietnamese community in North America, numbering an estimated 350,000 people.

camps: Camp Pendleton, California; Fort Chaffee, Arkansas; Fort Indiantown Gap, Pennsylvania; and Eglin Air Force Base, Florida. These facilities provided food, water, medical care, and education, as well as Buddhist and Roman Catholic religious services.

At the camps, Vietnamese refugees were interviewed and given medical exams. To help them adapt to life in their new country, they were offered courses on topics ranging from the English language, to American culture, to practical living skills such as finding a place to live, shopping, or obtaining a job. The instructors came from various governmental agencies and from private agencies and organizations. In many cases, volun-

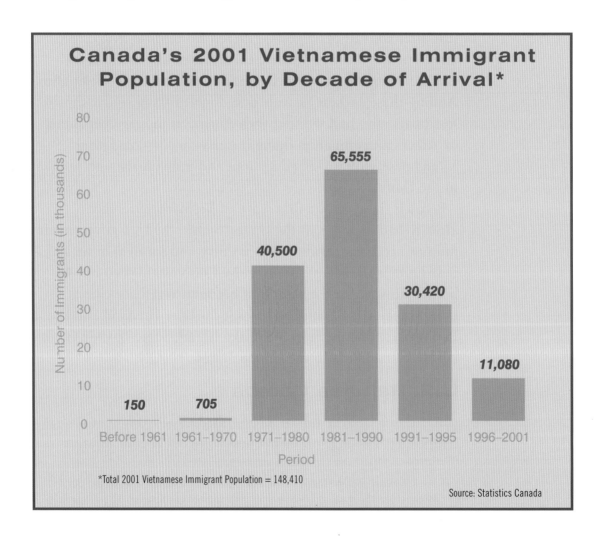

Canada's 2001 Vietnamese Immigrant Population, by Decade of Arrival*

Number of Immigrants (in thousands)

Before 1961	1961–1970	1971–1980	1981–1990	1991–1995	1996–2001
150	705	40,500	65,555	30,420	11,080

Period

*Total 2001 Vietnamese Immigrant Population = 148,410

Source: Statistics Canada

teers taught classes, provided medical care, and filled out paperwork.

Leaving the camp usually required sponsorship, although refugees who could already speak English and had $3,000 for each family member were allowed to exit the camp without a sponsor. Many Vietnamese who had worked for U.S. companies, such as airline companies, banks, or television networks and wire services, were rehired by their former employer and permitted to leave the camp.

Several national volunteer agencies, under contract from the U.S. Department of State, arranged sponsorships for the refugees, who were resettled throughout the country. The sponsor was responsible for helping the Vietnamese refugee—and, if applicable, his or her family members—find housing, jobs, and education. The sponsor also acted as a liaison to help the newcomers make the transition to life in the United States, by helping familiarize them with American customs.

Resettlement sponsors included individuals, families, community agencies, and religious organizations, especially Catholic and Protestant churches. The United States Catholic Conference, the Southern Baptist Convention, the Church World Service Organization, the Lutheran Church, and the International Rescue Committee were among the many organizations that donated funds, trained volunteers, and helped provide housing for the Vietnamese refugees.

By July 1975, the U.S. government had closed its refugee camps on Wake Island, Subic Bay, and Guam. By the following December, the camps within U.S. borders were also closed.

The Refugee Resettlement Process

Although Vietnamese refugees were no longer housed in U.S. camps, in order to enter the United States they still had to be sponsored, either by relatives or an organization. If refugees had extended family members already living in the United States, they were usually resettled in the area where the relatives lived. Otherwise, a resettlement agency acted as a sponsor, determining the refugees' ultimate destination based on jobs and services available in a given area. Resettled refugees were expected to establish residence there for a stipulated period of time.

The resettlement agency representative worked in partnership with church groups and volunteers from the community to provide clothing, food supplies, and furnishings for the newly arrived refugees. Through sponsorship programs, the newcomers would become connected with the community, familiarizing themselves with American customs, acquiring practical living skills, and taking advantage of government services and employment agencies.

Both governmental and nongovernmental organizations work together to help refugees. On the federal level, the Department of State provides funds to private agencies, which take care of welcoming and placement programs, providing services to refugees for their first 30 days in the United States. After that period, the Department of Health and Human Services (HHS) takes responsibility for long-term services, such as cash and medical assistance, and various social services. Within the HHS, the Office of Refugee Resettlement provides funding for refugee services programs through state governments as well as through private organizations.

Vietnamese Organizations

Refugee organizations, known as Mutual Assistance Associations, or MAAs, are private, nonprofit agencies whose members are typically Vietnamese immigrants who have permanently settled in the United States. Also called Vietnamese American organizations, they developed in 1975, soon after the first wave of Vietnamese refugees arrived in the country.

Funded by a combination of private and government money, MAAs help refugees adjust to life in America. The programs provide services such as job training, language instruction, and advice on getting access to government benefits. MAAs may serve as sponsors or simply as sources of information for the refugee. They also help newcomers hold on to old traditions, something of key importance for immigrants. Through the MAAs, refugees come together for Vietnamese holiday and cultural celebrations.

Another organization established in the late 1970s, the Southeast Asia Resource Action Center (SEARAC), developed in response to the need to help relocate the boat people. Called the Indochina Refugee Action Center (IRAC) when it was founded, the group later evolved into SEARAC. Among the organization's goals is to ensure that the voice of Southeast Asian immigrants is heard, particularly regarding government legislation and policies (such as welfare reform and naturalization policies) that may affect their lives. SEARAC also provides information to newcomers on a variety of topics, including education, health care, safety, economic development, and civil rights.

A national network of community-based organizations serving Vietnamese refugees operates in Canada. Founded in 1980, the Vietnamese Canadian Federation (VCF) is a nonprofit,

Viet-AID

Throughout North America, organizations provide assistance for Vietnamese immigrants. Most are centered in major metropolitan areas, where they serve local residents.

The Vietnamese population in the Boston metropolitan area finds support from an organization called the Vietnamese American Initiative for Development, or Viet-AID for short. Created in 1995 as the nation's only grassroots community development corporation founded by Vietnamese, Viet-AID helps Vietnamese immigrants living in Boston adjust to life in the United States.

Operated mostly by Vietnamese refugees and immigrants, Viet-AID was instrumental in the construction of a $4.6-million community center that opened in 2002 in Dorchester, Massachusetts—a poor and predominantly Vietnamese neighborhood of Boston. Designed to address the needs of the entire community, the center houses a child-care program, after-school activities, a senior center, and offices. Viet-AID helped the small community of approximately 11,000 Vietnamese organize to raise funds and obtain donations and grants to build the center.

community-based organization made up of member associations located across Canada. The VCF's goals are to connect its various member groups so they can better provide Vietnamese immigrants with ways of preserving and developing their cultural heritage. And at the same time, the organization works to foster the successful integration of the Vietnamese into Canadian politics and society.

Many Vietnamese organizations based upon members' specific interests or backgrounds have sprung up over the years. Groups such as the Vietnamese Doctors Association and the

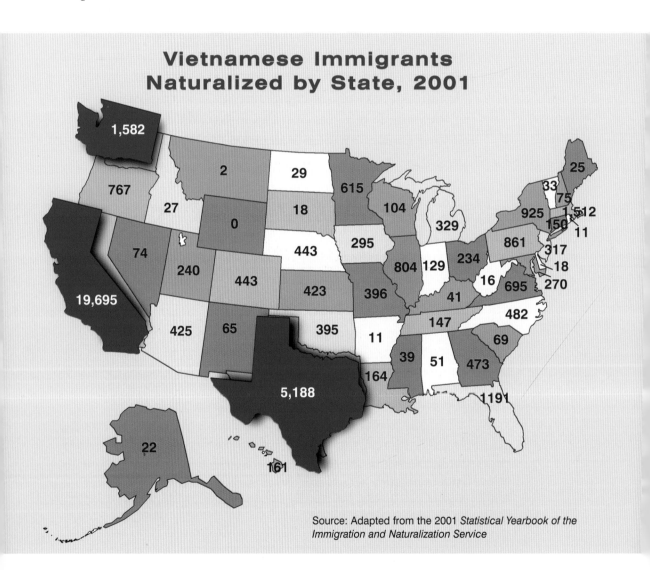

Vietnamese Immigrants Naturalized by State, 2001

Source: Adapted from the 2001 *Statistical Yearbook of the Immigration and Naturalization Service*

Vietnamese American Science and Professional Engineering Society (VASPES) give their members opportunities to network with other professionals. College and university campuses across the country host Vietnamese Student Associations. The National Association for the Education and Advancement of Cambodian, Laotian, and Vietnamese Americans (NAFEA) is a nonprofit organization serving Southeast Asian professionals, or those who work with Southeast Asians in the fields of education, social service, and community development.

Settling In

In 1975, the policy of the U.S. government was to settle small groups of Vietnamese refugees in communities located across the country. This strategy developed in order to prevent local governments from being overburdened with large numbers of refugees in need of many social services.

However, after living in a designated area for the required amount of time, many Vietnamese families chose to move so they could live closer to extended family members. Many migrated to communities located in or near urban areas. Like many new immigrants coming to a strange land, they chose to live in neighborhoods with people who spoke the same language and followed the same customs.

Today, the largest number of Vietnamese (approximately 40 percent) live in Southern California, particularly in Los Angeles and Orange County. In fact, Orange County is home to the largest Vietnamese population outside of Vietnam. In a suburb just south of Los Angeles sits Little Saigon, a Vietnamese community that is home to as many as 350,000 Vietnamese Americans.

Other large Vietnamese communities have developed in Southern California. The city of San Jose, located in the heart of Silicon Valley, has a population of about 125,000 Vietnamese, which makes it the second-largest Vietnamese enclave in the United States. Many Vietnamese Americans in San Jose work in its high-tech industries. Vietnamese immigrants in Los Angeles

County, California, have moved into parts of the city's Chinatown, where small Vietnamese businesses and shops have flourished.

Houston, Texas, with a Vietnamese population of about 100,000, lays claim to the title as the third-largest Vietnamese community in the United States. Nearby, Dallas also has a significant number of Vietnamese Americans. Several Vietnamese communities lie farther east in Louisiana, including New Orleans, where the first Vietnamese Catholic church was founded.

Vietnamese communities have sprouted in the metropolitan area of Washington, D.C., although its suburban neighborhood of Eden Center in Falls Church, Virginia, is considered the heart of the city's Vietnamese community. Significant numbers of Vietnamese also reside in the metropolitan areas of New York City; Richmond, Virginia; Atlantic City, New Jersey; and Boston, Massachusetts.

A significant number of Vietnamese Americans reside in the states of Washington, Pennsylvania, Minnesota, Massachusetts, New York, and Illinois. However it is the southern states of Texas, Virginia, Florida, Georgia, and Louisiana that account for about 30 percent of the Vietnamese population in the United States. And the western state of California claims about 50 percent of the Vietnamese population, recorded at almost half a million.

In Canada, most Vietnamese also tend to live in the cities or in metropolitan areas. More than half of the approximately 150,000 Vietnamese Canadians have settled in the province of Ontario, with the rest living in the provinces of Alberta, Quebec, and British Columbia. Many have migrated to urban areas of Toronto and Ottawa, Ontario; Montreal, Quebec; Edmonton and Calgary, Alberta; and Vancouver, British Columbia.

Finding Work

Among the first wave of newly arrived Vietnamese were tens of thousands of professionals, intellectuals, technicians, and

Los Angeles has one of the largest Chinatowns in the United States. A community of Vietnamese store-owners and other small business owners has thrived there for years.

skilled workers. Many tried to find the same kind of work they had in Vietnam, but jobs were scarce. Although most of these refugees were better educated and more familiar with the English language than those who came later, they still had to take jobs for which they were often overqualified.

Vietnamese newcomers needed income to survive—to put food on the table, to establish housing, to buy clothes. Many immigrants also hoped to save up to afford to bring other family members over from Vietnam, and so they willingly accepted whatever work they could find, often taking minimum-wage jobs and working long hours. They were eager to achieve a measure of financial stability in their new country, and willing to endure whatever hardships they might encounter. Both husband and wife, and often several members of the family, worked various jobs in order to pay expenses.

For example, Vietnamese-born immigrant Tony Lam, who in

1992 became a city councilman in Westminster, California, had a difficult start. He fled with his family in 1975, first to refugee camps in the Philippines and Guam, then to Florida, before finally arriving in Huntington Beach, California. In Vietnam, Lam and his brother had owned three large factories and done work for the U.S. Department of Defense. In California, however, one of his first jobs was pumping gas at a service station. His wife took a position packing boxes at a mail-order company.

Little Saigon

A city within a city, Little Saigon was carved out of a gritty, neglected area of a Los Angeles suburb during the late 1970s. Soon after the arrival of the first wave of refugees to nearby Camp Pendleton, numerous Vietnamese began to settle in the area. They quickly took advantage of government loans and grants to bring what had been a blighted neighborhood back to life. Homes and temples and family-run businesses sprouted, some buildings painted with the familiar pinks, blues, and greens commonly seen in Saigon—now called Ho Chi Minh City.

In 1988, the Westminster City Council passed a resolution to set aside an area, officially designated as Little Saigon, along Bolsa Avenue, between Ward and Magnolia Streets. According to a story in *Asia Week*, by 1996 this area of less than one square mile held "five banks, six major shopping centers, eight bakeries, and thousands of shops, cafes, restaurants, jewelry stores, hair salons, and professional offices in what is considered the largest Vietnamese business enclave outside of Vietnam."

In Little Saigon, billboards, signs, and storefronts are written in Vietnamese. Customers can shop and socialize in their native language, read Vietnamese papers, and listen to Vietnamese radio programs.

Estimates of the Vietnamese population in Little Saigon vary from 200,000 to 350,000. But the area draws thousands of outsiders as well. Today this Vietnamese enclave is the first stop for most recent immigrants, as well as a welcome retreat for longtime California residents living outside its borders. They journey to Little Saigon each weekend to eat and shop in hundreds of establishments owned or operated by Vietnamese Americans. "This is my home away from home," said Tracy Pham, a 49-year-old software consultant, to reporter for the *New York Times*. "When I am at work, I am an American. When I head back to Little Saigon, I'm 100 percent Vietnamese."

Still, by 1984, Lam and his family had saved enough to open the first of what would eventually become four restaurants.

A large number of new Vietnamese refugees worked jobs unrelated to their ability and background. Many took low-skilled jobs as convenience store clerks, short-order cooks, or janitors. Later, after graduating from English courses and job training classes, many worked their way up from entry-level business positions to better-paying jobs. Former merchants saved their wages, eventually accumulating enough to open up and once again run small businesses. Experienced Vietnamese fishermen migrated with their families to ports along the Gulf of Mexico in the United States or to the U.S. and Canadian Pacific coasts, where they could do similar work.

Vietnamese immigrants may take low-paying manual-labor jobs to help out family members in the United States as well as those who may still live in Vietnam.

Today, Vietnamese Americans and Vietnamese Canadians are employed in all sectors of the economy. They may work as fishers or farmers, or as hairdressers, florists, or acupuncturists. Some are entrepreneurs who have opened up shops ranging from small grocery stores to travel agencies to major manufacturing firms. Others entered the medical field and have become doctors or dentists. Still others work in universities or companies as professors, researchers, scientists, engineers, or administrators.

5 Accepting Change, Keeping Traditions

For many Vietnamese, particularly those who came during the 1970s and 80s, just getting to the United States was a major accomplishment. A combination of determination, ingenuity, and a great deal of luck helped them make it to their new homeland. However, after arriving they faced the difficult challenge in adapting their lifestyle and customs to Western culture. For the most part, the Vietnamese have assimilated (become part of) American mainstream society fairly well as they share many values of Western society, particularly the importance of family and faith; being part of a community; and a strong work ethic, both in schools and in the workplace.

Strong Family Ties

Once settled in North America, most Vietnamese continued to follow the traditions and beliefs that were part of their way of life in Vietnam. Of central importance is the family, which in Vietnam is the foundation of social structure. The family acts as a unit: its members come to the aid of one another, providing assistance for the sick or needy, without question. On the other hand, when one member prospers, he or she is expected to share that wealth.

In Vietnam, extended families consisting of three or four generations often live together under one roof; the married couple lives with the husband's parents. If they do not live together,

◀ A group of Vietnamese American third graders recites the Pledge of Allegiance in an elementary school in Little Saigon, California. The Vietnamese are known for having a strong work ethic, which has enabled them to succeed in American society while still holding on to some of the homeland's customs and lifestyles.

extended families tend to live close to one another, even after children have married and moved into their own houses.

In Vietnam, the traditional Vietnamese family is a patriarchal hierarchy in which the father seeks to maintain strict authority over the rest of the family members. Decisions that affect the fortunes of the family are often made by the oldest men. The respect given to men, especially older men, is very important according to Vietnamese custom.

The welfare of the family holds more importance than the desires of individual members, a concept that often differs from American values. However, this "team" attitude in which several family members work together has helped many low-income Vietnamese families achieve financial security through the establishment of family-owned businesses.

Author and law professor Lan Cao grew up part of a typical extended Vietnamese family, which she described in a 1999 story for *Duke Law Magazine*. After immigrating to northern Virginia, everyone in the family contributed to saving up for the future. One uncle worked at a bowling alley, another at a hotel. As a teenager, Cao sold ice cream and worked at the local restaurant. "All of the money [we made] was for the pool," she explained. "I didn't keep the money I earned. It never occurred to me that it was mine." Eventually the family had pooled enough money to afford starting up a Vietnamese grocery and later, a dry cleaner.

Maintaining Religious Faith

In unified Vietnam, freedom of religion was repressed for many years under the communist regime. However, before 1976, the Vietnamese had been exposed to several different religions, including Buddhism, Confucianism, Catholicism, Taoism, and animism (the belief in good and evil spirits in the natural world). Many Vietnamese have combined elements of these religions in both their worship and day-to-day behavior.

More than half of the Vietnamese follow Buddhism, a faith based on the teachings of Gautama Buddha. Buddhists believe

It is typical for Vietnamese immigrants to burn incense in remembrance of dead relatives. Many immigrant families perform this ritual at altars in their homes, where they may also say prayers amd make food offerings.

that one's good acts will be rewarded in the next life, when one is reincarnated, or reborn to live another life. Buddhists do not believe in the value of pride, but rather that one should show only humility. Life should be lived in moderation, and one should remain unattached to material things. Vietnamese Buddhists living in North America worship, celebrate weddings, and perform funeral rites in temples that also serve as centers for community ceremonies, social gatherings, and cultural life.

Many Vietnamese Buddhists also follow certain beliefs of Confucianism and Taoism, and try to follow the teachings of these faiths as well. The Vietnamese concept of family loyalty stems from Confucianism, a philosophy originating from China. Confucianism holds that a hierarchy of authority must be observed for true social order to exist. Children are expected to show respect to their parents and their elders, and to look after their elders' welfare.

Confucianism also holds that this respect for one's elders should continue after their death. In other words, the family consists not only of the living, but also of the spirits of the dead. According to this belief, many Vietnamese honor deceased family members through ancestor worship. Traditional Vietnamese homes in North America have a place set aside for an altar, where during holidays and other special occasions, respect is shown by burning incense, saying prayers, and making food offerings.

The Chinese religion of Taoism promotes humility, as well as charity, simplicity, and patience. Taoism stresses the need for harmony and an appreciation, love, and respect for the natural world. Many Vietnamese who practice Taoism seek calmness and try to avoid disagreements.

Christianity is the second major religion of the North American Vietnamese community. Although Roman Catholics make up only about 8 percent of Vietnam's population, an esti-mated 30 to 40 percent of the Vietnamese population living in North America report they are Roman Catholics. They are able to hold services in Vietnamese since many of their priests came to North America as refugees as well. One of these priests, Father Dominic Mai Thanh Luong, founded the first Vietnamese American Roman Catholic church, in New Orleans, Louisiana.

The intermingling of various belief systems has given rise to two other religious groups in Vietnam: the Hoa Hao and the Cao Dai. Hoa Hao is similar to Buddhism, but focuses on indi-vidual, not temple, worshiping practices. Cao Dai combines elements of Buddhism, Confucianism, Taoism, and Roman Catholicism.

Celebrating Vietnamese Holidays

The dates of Vietnamese holidays differ from year to year because they follow the lunar calendar, in which each month is determined according to the phases of the moon.

One of the most important holidays for the Vietnamese celebrates the beginning of the year. The Vietnamese New Year, *Tet Nguyen Dan*, literally means "the first morning of the first day of the new period." Tet, as it is usually called, is a time for family gatherings and visits with friends. Many Vietnamese believe that what happens during this holiday will determine events for the coming year, and that the luck carried by the New Year's first visitor to a family's home will affect its future. To make sure that they are blessed with good luck, families will often invite someone important as their first visitor. And to ensure that the year is a peaceful one, adults avoid arguments and children stay on their best behavior.

Tet begins on the first day of the first month of the lunar calendar, and usually falls between January 19 and February 20. In Vietnam the date also marks the beginning of spring. In preparation for the celebrations, Vietnamese families clean their homes, decorate with flowers, and hang banners with wishes for happiness and prosperity. In rural Vietnam families erect a bamboo tree called a Cay Neu in front of the home. The Cay Neu is decorated with amulets or red paper (the color red is believed to ward off evil spirits).

Many of these traditions have carried over to life in North America, where refugees and immigrants celebrate their Vietnamese heritage during Tet by remembering the past, celebrating the new, and looking toward the future. Children receive presents of *li xi*, small red envelopes containing money. And families remember their ancestors with prayers and offerings placed on altars decorated with flowers and photographs of the deceased. A portion of a traditional Tet dinner is left on the altar for the family's ancestors, who are invited to join in the celebration. Traditional foods may include a whole chicken (symbolizing abundance and prosperity), *thit kho dua* (pork stew with hard-boiled eggs), and *banh chung* (a sticky rice cake filled with bean paste and pork).

Many large Vietnamese communities in North America hold

Tet festivals, often consisting of parades and fairs that may feature food bazaars, games, outdoor concerts, beauty pageants, martial arts competitions, and fashion shows. During a Tet festival participants dress in traditional clothes, and display traditional Vietnamese arts, including silk painting, pottery, and flower arranging. A space is always dedicated to honoring ancestors, where the Vietnamese pray and make offerings. The

A couple watches the glowing lanterns of the Mid-Autumn Festival, which usually takes place between mid-September and early October. The holiday is celebrated with parades, dances, and moon cakes. Its most well-known celebrations in the United States take place in the Vietnamese communities of San Jose and Washington, D.C.

festival gives immigrants and refugees the opportunity to celebrate their heritage together and maintain their connections to the community. It is also an occasion for Vietnamese immigrants to share their culture with the mainstream society of North America.

For older Vietnamese Americans, particularly those who escaped from their homeland, the commemoration of Tet can be a bittersweet event. While they find joy through celebrating their heritage, the event serves as a sad reminder of the country they left behind. Younger Vietnamese, however, tend to regard Tet celebrations differently, more as a symbol of their roots. In *The Vietnamese Experience in America*, author Paul Rutledge describes how Tran Vo, a Vietnamese American teenager living in the Midwest, appreciates the holiday:

> I like the Tet celebration. It is a time when we can party and have a good time together. I don't like some of the things with candles, incense, and all that, but I know it is important to my parents. I don't understand what it all means, but Tet is a way of just being Vietnamese. For my folks it is a way of remembering. For me it is a way of saying that that's kind of a part of me.

Another Vietnamese holiday particularly enjoyed by children is Tet Trung Thu, or the Mid-Autumn Festival. Held on the 15th day of the 8th lunar month, the Mid-Autumn Festival, which usually takes place between mid-September and early October, serves both as a harvest celebration and a time specially dedicated to children. In Vietnam children parade at night during the full moon, singing and carrying lighted lanterns shaped as moons, stars, fish, or butterflies. They may dance the traditional dragon or flower dance, and eat moon cakes filled with lotus seeds, ground beans, and orange peels. Vietnamese communities in Washington, D.C., and San Jose are particularly known for their Mid-Autumn Festival celebrations.

Vietnamese immigrants and refugees may observe several other holidays reflecting their heritage or faith. The Trung Sisters Day honors the bravery of two Vietnamese women who in around A.D. 40 valiantly rallied the people to drive out Chinese invaders. The holiday falls on the sixth day of the second lunar month, usually in late February or early March. The National Founders' Day, also known as Hung Kings Day, commemorates the founding of Vietnam by the Hung Kings. It takes place on the tenth day of the third lunar month, around April 19. Buddha's birthday, also known as the Illumination, celebrates not only the birth of the religion's founder but also his enlightenment and death. The holiday falls on the eighth day of the fourth lunar month, usually in early May. Celebrated on the 15th day of the 7th lunar month, the Day of the Dead (also known as All Souls' Day) is a special occasion for Vietnamese to remember their dead ancestors by visiting their graves and making food offerings.

Scattered Settlement

Throughout the history of immigration, newcomers have often relied on an existing community of immigrants in their new homeland to help make the difficult transition to their new life. However, before 1975, no such community existed for the Vietnamese in North America. As a result, the first Vietnamese arrivals in the U.S. had only each other to rely on for support.

It took some time for Vietnamese immigrant communities to develop, since the U.S. government followed an objective to not resettle large clusters of refugees in a single community. Refugees were sent to all 50 states; even Alaska received 81 refugees. While this policy of scattered settlement had some benefits, it also served to isolate many Vietnamese, who sometimes discovered they were the only nonwhite citizens in their community.

Eventually, many Vietnamese families moved from where they first settled, and numerous Vietnamese communities sprang up within cities and their outlying suburbs. Today many of these communities serve as places where Vietnamese and non-Vietnamese alike can enjoy Vietnamese culture.

Importance of Education

The educated class has always been held in great esteem and given a special place in Vietnamese society. The emphasis on learning has remained with many Vietnamese refugees and immigrants, whose children often do well academically because of their parents' high expectations. Education is strongly valued by most Asian immigrant groups, a fact reflected by their numbers graduating high school. In fact, according to the 2000 U.S. Census, of all groups the Asian/Pacific Islanders had the highest rate of graduation from high school—94.6 percent.

6 CHALLENGES TO OVERCOME

Because of their strong work ethic and dedicated perseverance, Vietnamese Americans have overcome many of the obstacles that can prevent immigrants from achieving success in their new homeland. Learning the language, finding a job and a place to live, fighting in the face of prejudice, and establishing community roots took time but was eventually accomplished. Other problems, such as generational differences and changes in the ways of the traditional family, persist even today.

Difficulties with Language

Learning the English language is quite difficult for many Vietnamese. Their language contains six principle tones; the same word has a different meaning depending on the tone in which it is spoken. For example, the word *ma* means "ghost" when spoken in a level tone, "check" when spoken in a breathy rising tone, or "but" when said in a breathy falling tone. English is not a tonal language, and its vocabulary is larger than that of any other language in the world. For many Vietnamese, these differences are a great impediment to developing fluency.

It is common for newcomers to North America who are still learning English to be frustrated about their inability to communicate. Without an interpreter, a visit to the doctor's office or to a government agency can be stressful and confusing. Often

◀ A Vietnamese man studies for his U.S. citizenship test. Acquiring citizenship is one of many potential challenges for Vietnamese immigrants, along with learning English, overcoming prejudice, and adjusting to changes in the traditional family structure.

immigrant children who have learned to read, write, and speak English at school are called upon to translate for their non-English speaking parents. In the patriarchal culture of the Vietnamese, in which the grandfather and father hold authority, having to transfer this control to the children can be disorienting.

Vietnamese who enter the United States with a basic knowledge of the English language are able to get jobs and establish financial stability more quickly. But life is typically harder for those who can not read or write English. They can not obtain jobs easily when they are unable to communicate with potential employers, and if they do find jobs, it is often not steady or meaningful work.

A man stands in front of a Vietnamese community center that was vandalized in a racist attack. American prejudice against the Vietnamese is less prevalent today than it was in the 1970s, when the losses of the Vietnam War and an economic recession helped influence mixed responses toward incoming refugees.

Combating Prejudice

In 1975, when Saigon fell to the communists, public opinion polls showed that slightly more than half of all Americans—about 54 percent—were opposed to allowing Vietnamese refugees to live in the United States. About 36 percent were in favor, while the rest expressed no opinion one way or another. Many U.S. citizens believed that the United States had a moral obligation to provide a safe haven for the Vietnamese.

The Vietnam War deeply divided the citizens of the United States. Some believed the government needed to become involved in the conflict in order to stop the spread of communism, while others thought the government had no business meddling in the affairs of a country halfway around the world. When newly arriving Vietnamese immigrants began moving into their neighborhoods, Americans remained divided on how to treat them. Some people rushed to help the newcomers become established; others viewed the foreigners with resentment or suspicion.

In some communities the arrival of the first waves of Vietnamese in the 1970s sparked friction with longtime residents. The U.S. was in the midst of a deep economic recession at the time, and some Americans complained that the Vietnamese refugees were taking their jobs away.

Some Vietnamese encountered racial prejudice in finding jobs and places to live. One of the most visible conflicts occurred along the Gulf Coast, where Vietnamese fishermen began competing with local shrimpers. In Texas, Vietnamese shrimpers angered the residents by unwittingly breaking unwritten rules, such as fishing in areas already claimed by others or using illegal nets. Hostilities between Vietnamese and Texan fishermen escalated, and Vietnamese fishing nets were cut, boats were burned, and homes were firebombed. Some refugees moved away, but most stood their ground.

Eventually, the two sides worked out their differences. Despite the conflicts, the Vietnamese had earned grudging respect from the locals for their work ethic, skill, and motivation.

Changes in the Family

The transition to life in a Western culture was the catalyst for many changes to the traditional Vietnamese family, especially in terms of gender roles, family expectations, and family relationships.

The Vietnam War and subsequent emigration from Vietnam had already forced many Vietnamese women to assume new responsibilities as head of the household. In families where the husbands left for years at a time to join the fighting, or where family members were separated during the chaos of escaping from Vietnam, the mother had to make decisions. After being resettled in their new homeland, many families looked to the

An Immigrant's Poem

My children forget
that I am head of home in America
as I was in Vietnam.
My children do not obey
my requests
and think I am without the new wisdom
they have learned in America.
I have the old wisdom.

My children forget
the teaching of our ways,
of what their father once taught them,
of life in Vietnam.
Too much television, too much music.
They tell me always,
I am in America.
My children change
and I do not change.
My children forget
me.

  —Vietnamese woman from Dallas, Texas

Source: Tenhula, John. *Voices from Southeast Asia: The Refugee Experience in the United States* (Ellis Island Series).

Because a greater percentage of Vietnamese women have joined the American workforce than in their home country, the traditional structure of the Vietnamese immigrant family has faced changes. Some Vietnamese men have felt uncomfortable with Western attitudes toward gender roles.

mothers to take charge, a responsibility that some hardly felt prepared to assume. Even in families that remained intact, many resettled Vietnamese men found themselves uncomfortable with Western society's attitudes toward the two genders.

Other factors made the transition to life in Western society difficult, particularly for Vietnamese men. A loss of social status, compounded by feelings of inadequacy due to economic insecurity, sometimes contributed to depression. Severe cases led to family problems such as marital troubles, spousal abuse, and substance abuse. Such troubles sometimes went unresolved, because Vietnamese tradition dictates that individuals rely primarily on the family, not on mental health professionals.

Youth Crime

While Vietnamese youth have made tremendous contributions to America's schools, in some cases the breakdown of the traditional Vietnamese family has left its younger members at loose ends, particularly newcomers who already felt isolated from family and community. At particular risk have been school-age refugees and immigrants who struggle with adjusting to their new society. Because of problems speaking the language, some of them have dropped out of school or failed to obtain work. Some have found solace with other youth like themselves and have become members of gangs.

Starting with the influx of boat people in 1979, a number of youth gangs, consisting of members aged 12 to 25, have developed. During the 1980s these gangs were fairly small, consisting of about eight to ten members. In 2000, reports indicated that some Vietnamese gangs claimed over 1,000 members. Past surveys of Vietnamese living in California have shown that a large majority identify gangs as the biggest threat to their communities.

Old Values vs. New Beliefs

Like all immigrant families, the children find themselves growing up in two worlds—that of their parents' homeland and that of Western society. Many immigrant children find themselves torn between the cultures of both. The millions of Vietnamese living in North America are no exception. On one hand, they may find their life in the United States to be a source of great pride and satisfaction; at other times it can be frustrating trying to balance Vietnamese customs with American or Canadian ways.

In many Vietnamese immigrant families, the language, food, and customs at home are Vietnamese. Away from home, particularly in school, Vietnamese children are exposed to another world with a different language and cultural aspects that some times contradict that of the traditional Vietnamese.

Most children of immigrants do not want to appear to be different from their American friends. One way that many Vietnamese children adapt to Western culture is to change their given name to a similar-sounding American one. For instance, a boy called "Tien" at home could be called "Tim" when he is among friends.

In fact, Vietnamese immigrants often have already "Americanized" their names by changing the order of their two names. In Vietnam, the family name comes first, followed by the middle and then the personal, or given name. For example, the name Nguyen Van Nam may appear in Western culture as "Nam Van Nguyen."

Some Vietnamese parents even encourage their children to change their Vietnamese-sounding given names to American ones. In a *Time* magazine story on the children of immigrants, Vietnamese refugee Le Giau told reporter Anastasia Toufexis, "They should change their names because it's easier for them when they go to work." Following his own advice, Le Giau changed the names of his three daughters—Hanh, Tien, and Trang—to Hannah, Christina, and Jennifer.

If a Vietnamese family owns a business, the children are usually expected to help out to ensure its success. As a result there often can be no time for activities with friends outside of school. Le Giau's family fits this scenario. His four children, aged 12 to 18, all help out at the family's pastry shop, which has often prevented them from accepting invitations to do

Vietnamese immigrant families are often challenged to find a balance between Vietnamese customs and American or Canadian ways. Parents may become discouraged when their children adopt new values that contradict the traditional values of the family.

things with American friends. Eighteen-year-old Hannah explained, "American children don't understand. They don't know why I can't go to the beach."

Many Vietnamese refugees have been troubled over the influence of Western society on their children. In Vietnam, a youth should be hardworking, responsible, and deferential to elders, who are honored for their wisdom and knowledge. Many older Vietnamese believe their children have lost respect for them because of the influence of American television, radio, and movies.

Disagreements between parents and children may range from arguments over appropriate haircuts, music, and clothing styles to receiving permission to date. In strongly traditional families dating is unheard of; so is divorce, which is much more common in North America than in Vietnam. And Vietnamese parents must go through a difficult period of adjustment when their children choose to move far away to attend school or work. As first-generation and second-generation Vietnamese children grow up in Western society, they have to make a hard decision between abiding by traditional ways and charting their own paths.

Controversy over Communism

One controversial area that divides many older and younger Vietnamese immigrants is politics. The older generation remains staunchly anti-communist, finding it difficult to forget the persecution they experienced. However, many members of the younger generations do not share their aversion to communism, having not directly suffered government injustices in Vietnam. They did not live through years in oppressive reeducation camps, attempted desperate escapes, or faced the horrendous conditions of refugee camps.

The communist symbols of present-day Vietnam remain an issue for many older Vietnamese Americans. In 1999 hundreds of demonstrators took to the streets of Little Saigon to protest a video store owner's display of a Ho Chi Minh poster and the

Communist Vietnamese flag. The same flag, which shows a large yellow five-pointed star in the center of a red background, was carried by North Vietnamese forces during the Vietnam War.

In August 2001, a Vietnamese group in San Jose, California, protested the U.S. Postal Service's use of the Vietnamese flag on multilingual brochures advertising the agency's services. A spokesman for the Vietnamese American Community of Northern California, Ky Ngo, told the Associated Press, "The Vietnamese refugees living in the United States came here seeking freedom from the communists. They violated our human rights, they oppressed us. So when we see the communist flag, we naturally get upset." The pamphlets, which had been distributed to 11,900 post offices, were removed and replaced with brochures without flags.

In early 2003 the U.S. State Department stepped in when Virginia state legislators introduced legislation that would have required the display of the former South Vietnamese flag instead of the current flag at official functions. The country of Vietnam protested strongly, calling such action an offense to its government. Ultimately the measure did not come to a vote.

Soon afterward, in February 2003, Westminster and Garden Grove City Councils in California both proposed and passed resolutions authorizing the use of the South Vietnamese flag at all of their official functions. They also banned any use of the communist flag. Although the current Vietnamese government protested these actions, and requested that the governor of California, Gray Davis, prevent the resolutions from going forward, his office responded that the city councils were within their rights to establish their own policies.

Overcoming Poverty

Asian Americans have one of the highest household incomes of any foreign-born group ($55,525 in 2000, compared with the median of $36,000), with only one-tenth living in poverty. However, the Vietnamese have a higher poverty rate, with a little

less than one-third of Vietnamese households living below the poverty level.

The higher poverty rate can be explained by the fact that at least one-third of Vietnamese immigrants in the United States are recent immigrants, having lived in America for less than 10 years. Many coming to North America today have only recently escaped from the poverty of their own country, and they have begun a new life with very little money.

The majority of Vietnamese in the United States were not born there. According to the 2000 census, approximately 863,000 foreign-born residents of the United States were from Vietnam, or 79 percent of the 1.1 million Vietnamese living in America at that time. Yet 88 percent of those who have lived in the country longer than 10 years have attained middle- or upper-class status. Such rapid progress is due in part to the great emphasis placed on education and achievement, a result of which is that the children of many Vietnamese families have moved into high-paying professional, managerial, and entrepreneurial jobs.

Vietnamese Americans of Little Saigon speak out against a neighbor's display of the Communist Vietnamese flag in the window of his video store, February 1999. Some Vietnamese Americans believe the flag is a painful reminder of the abuses committed by the North Vietnamese before and after unification.

Returning Home

The Viet Kieu, the name for Vietnamese who return to their homeland after living in the United States, have made a great impression on the economy and the younger generations of Vietnam. In any given year, some 100,000 Vietnamese Americans return to visit or do business in Vietnam. Their presence has helped transform the lifestyle of younger Vietnamese still living in the country.

After almost two decades, the normalization of relations between the U.S. and Vietnamese governments in 1994 led to a flood of visiting native-born Vietnamese. Their presence has benefited the Vietnamese government, and it also has been a source of concern. The money the Viet Kieu has spent has provided a significant boost to the country's sagging economy; on the other hand, the government is afraid that their progressive attitudes and politics may bring about change that will affect the country forever.

This flow of Vietnamese back to their homeland has served to divide the country somewhat. Southern Vietnam enjoys most of the economic benefits of the relationship as more than $2 billion a year is sent back to family members from ethnic Vietnamese living in North America. That is twice the amount of foreign aid that the Vietnamese government receives each year.

7 FULFILLING HOPES AND DREAMS

Between 1990 and 2000, the Vietnamese population in the United States almost doubled in size, and in 2000 it surpassed the one million mark. In Canada the number of people reporting Vietnamese descent grew as well, passing 136,000 in 1996 and then reaching almost 148,000 in 2002. North America continues to see large-scale immigration as tens of thousands of Vietnamese immigrants continue to arrive each year.

Anxieties About the Future

Many older generations of Vietnamese Americans remain concerned about the future of the Vietnamese in North America. Some fear the dissolution of the family, which has been a vital component of Vietnamese society for thousands of years.

Others worry that the younger generations will become too assimilated to Western culture, at the cost of losing their heritage. Again, it is mostly older people who believe that moving to North America has caused the abandonment of customs and social etiquette unique to Vietnam. They complain, for instance, that not enough young people are learning to speak Vietnamese.

In *Changing Identities: Vietnamese Americans, 1975–1995*, author James M. Freeman presents the point of view of a Vietnamese-born refugee, Colonel Tran Dinh Bui, who sees that such change is inevitable.

"Great changes have occurred in Vietnam over the past 100

◀ A naturalized Vietnamese American displays his U.S. passport. With the Vietnamese population in the United States surpassing one million in 2000, a large group of Vietnamese will likely become permanent residents and acquire U.S. citizenship in the years ahead.

years, but there the Vietnamese were the majority in their homeland," Tran said. "Here in America, we are a minority that will be absorbed. The first two generations of Vietnamese in America will maintain Vietnamese traditions; the generation of my grandchildren will not."

Improved U.S.–Vietnamese Relations

It has been many years since the end of the Vietnam War, and relations between the United States and the Vietnamese government have improved considerably. However, the idea of the United States being on friendly terms with communist Vietnam is controversial for many Vietnamese. Most refugees remain fiercely opposed to renewing ties, while their children are more receptive to opening up economic and cultural opportunities between the two countries. Some have traveled to Vietnam, or wish to do so, in order to learn more about their identity.

After lifting its trade embargo against Vietnam in 1994, the U.S. government established diplomatic relations with the communist

President Bill Clinton greets Vietnamese field workers during his trip in November 2000, the first visit by an American president since 1976. The United States and Vietnam have enjoyed improved relations since 1994, when the U.S. government lifted a long-standing trade embargo.

government the following year. In 2000 the two countries signed a treaty establishing normal bilateral trade relations, which was ratified and came into effect in 2001. Around the same time, the U.S. government pledged $1.7 million to help the Vietnamese government find and destroy thousands of unexploded mines that had been buried throughout the country.

Perhaps the most significant event, however, was President Bill Clinton's trip to Vietnam in November 2000, when he became the first American president to visit the country since its unification in 1976. During his trip, Clinton spoke at Vietnam National University, in Hanoi. In his speech he supported the building of a partnership with Vietnam:

> We [the U.S. government] are . . . eager to build our partnership with Vietnam. We believe it's good for both our nations. We believe the Vietnamese people have the talent to succeed in this new global age as they have in the past.
>
> We know it because we've seen the progress you have made in this last decade. We have seen the talent and ingenuity of the Vietnamese who have come to settle in America. Vietnamese-Americans have become elected officials, judges, and leaders in science and in our high-tech industry. [In 1999] a Vietnamese American achieved a mathematical breakthrough that will make it easier to conduct high-quality video-conferencing. And all America took notice when Hoang Nhu Tran graduated number one in his class at the United States Air Force Academy.
>
> Vietnamese-Americans have flourished not just because of their unique abilities and their good values, but also because they have had the opportunity to make the most their abilities and their values. . . .

Improvements to Vietnam's economy have come slowly, and the poor have few options but to try to leave. The normalization of relations with the United States will make it easier for Vietnamese citizens to reunite with family members living overseas, and use the opportunity to leave poverty conditions behind. Both factors—Vietnam's poverty and the desire for family reunification—are likely to keep immigration to the United States at a high level. It is estimated that by 2010, Vietnamese Americans may surpass all Asian groups in the United States, except the Chinese.

Vietnamese in Public Service

Vietnamese Americans, and Asian Americans in general, have not had a strong leadership presence in American politics. The Vietnamese are the only Asian immigrant group that identifies more often with the Republican Party than the Democratic Party. This tendency is likely the result of the group's more conservative views on certain issues, including foreign policy toward communist countries.

Since 1903, there have been 33 members of Congress of Asian and Pacific Islander descent. As of 2003 only nine Asian Americans were members of Congress (seven in the House of Representatives and two in the Senate). However, these num-

The Growing Influence of Vietnamese in the Catholic Church

Although the Vietnamese are a small minority among immigrants to the United States, they are making a strong impression on the nation's Catholic Church. While only about 8 percent of the Vietnamese in Vietnam are Roman Catholic, as many as 40 percent of the refugees who came to the United States follow this faith.

As of 2000, less than 1 percent, or 300,000, of the estimated 61 million Catholics in the United States claimed Vietnamese descent. However, a significantly larger proportion of men studying for the priesthood—nearly 3 percent—are Vietnamese American.

The presence of Vietnamese Catholics has resulted in new parishes and missions throughout New Orleans, Louisiana. Strong Vietnamese Catholic communities can also be found in Houston, Texas; San Jose, California; and Orange County, California. (In April 2003, the Orange County diocese welcomed the nation's first Vietnamese Roman Catholic bishop, Dominic Dinh Mai Luong.)

In Carthage, Missouri, a monastery belonging to the Congregation of the Mother Co-Redemptrix, a Vietnamese order, draws tens of thousands of Vietnamese families to an annual religious and social gathering each August. In a weeklong celebration known as Marian Days, Vietnamese Catholics celebrate masses and give thanksgiving, meet with friends and relatives, and march in a procession of thousands.

bers look to increase in the future as the Asian American population in the United States continues to grow.

Vietnamese Americans, most of whom have become part of the American community only in the past few decades, are only just beginning to make inroads into American politics. There are only a few prominent Vietnamese Americans in high political positions. Among them is Tony Lam, who became the first Vietnamese to hold elected office in the United States when he was elected to the Westminster City Council in California. Judge Thang Nguyen Barrett, who also holds office in California, was the first Vietnamese superior court judge.

Within the federal government, Nguyen Ngoc Bich served as acting director for the Office of Bilingual Education during the administration of President George H. W. Bush, while several more Vietnamese Americans were tapped for important positions within the administration of President George W. Bush. They include John Quoc Duong, the executive director of the White House Initiative on Asian Americans and Pacific Islanders; Mina Nguyen, a special assistant to U.S. Labor Secretary Elaine Chao, and Viet Dinh, formerly assistant attorney general overseeing the Office of Legal Policy in the U.S. Department of Justice.

The Vietnamese are still relatively new arrivals to North America. As other immigrants have found, it takes time to become part of the culture and to cultivate an ethnic identity within society. However in a relatively short amount of time—just a few decades—Vietnamese Americans have made great progress and have much to be proud of. They have been honored for excellence in a variety of fields, including education, science, social services, business, and politics. As Vietnamese Americans continue to become actively involved in life in the United States and Canada, they will continue to earn respect. The values that served their ancestors so well in Vietnam—perseverance and the ability to overcome adversity—will serve them just as well in their new homeland.

FAMOUS VIETNAMESE AMERICANS/CANADIANS

Thang Nguyen Barrett (1961–), first Vietnamese American judge to sit on a court of general jurisdiction, becoming judge of the superior court of Santa Clara, California, in 1997. He has also served on the board of directors of the Center for Southeast Asian Refugee Resettlement.

Nguyen Ngoc Bich (ca. 1938–), educator, author, teacher, translator, and director of the Vietnamese Service at Radio Free Asia; known for his work for human rights and democracy within Vietnam.

Lan Cao (1963–), novelist and professor of law. Her *Monkey Bridge*, published in 1997, was the first novel by a Vietnamese American to be released by a major publishing house.

Kieu Chinh (1941–), actress; has appeared in more than 70 television shows, such as *M*A*S*H*, and movies, such as *The Joy Luck Club* (1993) and *Green Dragon* (2002).

John Quoc Duong (1973–), executive director of the White House Initiative on Asian Americans and Pacific Islanders.

Le Ly Hayslip (1949–), author of autobiographical memoir *When Heaven and Earth Changed Places*; founder of the East Meets West Foundation, a humanitarian relief organization serving children and their families in Vietnam.

Andrew Lam (ca. 1964–), associate editor at Pacific News Service, in San Francisco; short story writer and regular commentator for National Public Radio's *All Things Considered*.

Dominic Mai Thanh Luong (1940–), first Vietnamese Roman Catholic bishop; founder of the first Vietnamese American Catholic church, Mary Queen of Vietnam Church, located in New Orleans, Louisiana.

Navia Nguyen (1973–), fashion supermodel who has also had small television and film roles; voted one of the "50 Most Beautiful" in *People* magazine in 1996.

Kien Duc Trung Pham (ca. 1958–), founder of Vietnam Forum Foundation, which provides educational and humanitarian support to Vietnam.

Eugene Huu-Chau Trinh (1950–), first Vietnamese American astronaut; crew member on 1992 mission of the space shuttle *Columbia*.

GLOSSARY

Amerasian—a person of mixed American and Asian descent.

asylee—a person who receives asylum.

asylum—a grant to stay in a country. In the case of the United States an individual can receive asylum if he or she proves a well-founded fear of persecution.

communist—a follower of communism; relating to a repressive political system in which most or all property is owned by the state and is intended to be equally distributed.

doi moi—Vietnamese for "new change" or "renewal"; economic program introduced by Vietnamese government that allowed private control over previously state-owned businesses and operations.

embargo—to stop or limit trade to foreign countries.

ethnic—having a common racial, tribal, religious, or cultural background.

exodus—emigration involving a large number of people.

green card—immigrant visa that allows an immigrant to work legally, travel abroad and return, and become eligible for citizenship.

guerrilla—a fighter using unconventional warfare.

Indochina—the Southeast Asian region comprised of the countries of Cambodia, Laos, and Vietnam.

refugee—person forced to leave his or her homeland due to war or political persecution.

repatriate—to bring or send back a person to his or her own native country.

United Nations High Commission for Refugees—A UN organization established in 1950 to help refugees around the world; for the Vietnamese, the UNHCR helped set up refugee camps, provide food and supplies, and resettle refugees.

Viet Cong—Ho Chi Minh's guerrilla forces in former South Vietnam.

Viet Kieu—Vietnamese who return to their homeland after living in the United States.

Vietminh—communist forces loyal to Ho Chi Minh.

FURTHER READING

Chanoff, David, and Doan Van Toai. *Vietnam: A Portrait of Its People at War.* New York: I.B. Tauris, 1996.

Do, Hien Duc. *The Vietnamese Americans*. Westport, Conn.: Greenwood Press, 1999.

Freeman, James M. *Changing Identities: Vietnamese Americans, 1975–1995*. Boston: Allyn and Bacon, 1995.

Lam, Lawrence. *From Being Uprooted to Surviving*. Toronto: York Lanes Press, 1996.

Pham, Andrew X. *Catfish and Mandala: A Two-Wheeled Voyage Through the Landscape and Memory of Vietnam*. New York: Farrar, Straus and Giroux, 1999.

Rutledge, James Paul. *The Vietnamese Experience in America*. Bloomington: Indiana University Press, 1992.

Springstubb, Tricia. *The Vietnamese Americans*. San Diego, Calif.: Lucent Books, 2002

Tenhula, John. *Voices from Southeast Asia: The Refugee Experience in the United States*. New York: Holmes and Meier Publishers, 1991.

Zia, Helen. *Asian American Dreams: The Emergence of an American People*. New York: Farrar, Straus and Giroux, 2000.

INTERNET RESOURCES

http://www.boatpeople.com

The Boat People Connection is dedicated to the memories and legacy of the Vietnamese Boat People, and the website allows survivors to share their own recollections of their escape.

http://www.vietnamembassy-usa.org

The home site of the Embassy of the Socialist Republic of Vietnam, located in Washington, D.C.

http://www.vietfederation.ca/

The Vietnamese Canadian Federation (VCF) is a resource network of Vietnamese organizations in Canada.

http://www.viethorizons.com/

Viet Horizons is a weekly English-language radio show for Vietnamese Americans. This homepage includes audio recordings of interviews with prominent Vietnamese Americans.

http://www.vwip.org

The Vietnam War Internet Project contains information and documents about the various Indochina Wars, including oral histories and memoirs of those who participated in or protested against the conflicts.

http://viettouch.com

Viettouch is a resource for Vietnamese art, history, literature, music, and other forms of cultural expression.

INDEX

Numbers in **bold italic** refer to captions.

INDEX

INDEX

CONTRIBUTORS

SENATOR EDWARD M. KENNEDY has represented Massachusetts in the United States Senate for more than forty years. Kennedy serves on the Senate Judiciary Committee, where he is the senior Democrat on the Immigration Subcommittee. He currently is the ranking member on the Health, Education, Labor and Pensions Committee in the Senate, and also serves on the Armed Services Committee, where he is a member of the Senate Arms Control Observer Group. He is also a member of the Congressional Friends of Ireland and a trustee of the John F. Kennedy Center for the Performing Arts in Washington, D.C.

Throughout his career, Kennedy has fought for issues that benefit the citizens of Massachusetts and the nation, including the effort to bring quality health care to every American, education reform, raising the minimum wage, defending the rights of workers and their families, strengthening the civil rights laws, assisting individuals with disabilities, fighting for cleaner water and cleaner air, and protecting and strengthening Social Security and Medicare for senior citizens.

Kennedy is the youngest of nine children of Joseph P. and Rose Fitzgerald Kennedy, and is a graduate of Harvard University and the University of Virginia Law School. His home is in Hyannis Port, Massachusetts, where he lives with his wife, Victoria Reggie Kennedy, and children, Curran and Caroline. He also has three grown children, Kara, Edward Jr., and Patrick, and four grandchildren.

Senior consulting editor STUART ANDERSON served as Executive Associate Commissioner for Policy and Planning and Counselor to the Commissioner at the Immigration and Naturalization Service from August 2001 until January 2003. He spent four and a half years on Capitol Hill on the Senate Immigration Subcommittee, first for Senator Spencer Abraham and then as Staff Director of the subcommittee for Senator Sam Brownback. Prior to that, he was Director of Trade and Immigration Studies at the Cato Institute in Washington, D.C., where he produced reports on the history of immigrants in the military and the role of immigrants in high technology. He currently serves as Executive Director of the National Foundation for American Policy, a nonpartisan public policy research organization focused on trade, immigration, and international relations. He has an M.A. from Georgetown University and a B.A. in Political Science from Drew University. His articles have appeared in such publications as the *Wall Street Journal*, *New York Times*, and *Los Angeles Times*.

MARIAN L. SMITH served as the senior historian of the U.S. Immigration and Naturalization Service (INS) from 1988 to 2003, and is currently the immigration and naturalization historian within the Department of Homeland Security in Washington, D.C. She studies, publishes, and speaks on the history of the immigration agency and is active in management of official 20th-century immigration records.

PETER HAMMERSCHMIDT is the First Secretary (Financial and Military Affairs) for the Permanent Mission of Canada to the United Nations. Before taking this position, he was a ministerial speechwriter and policy specialist for the Department of National

Defence in Ottawa. Prior to joining the public service, he served as the Publications Director for the Canadian Institute of Strategic Studies in Toronto. He has a B.A. (Honours) in Political Studies from Queen's University, and an MScEcon in Strategic Studies from the University of Wales, Aberystwyth. He currently lives in New York, where in his spare time he operates a freelance editing and writing service, Wordschmidt Communications.

Manuscript reviewer ESTHER OLAVARRIA serves as General Counsel to Senator Edward M. Kennedy, ranking Democrat on the U.S. Senate Judiciary Committee, Subcommittee on Immigration. She is Senator Kennedy's primary advisor on immigration, nationality, and refugee legislation and policies. Prior to her current job, she practiced immigration law in Miami, Florida, working at several non-profit organizations. She cofounded the Florida Immigrant Advocacy Center and served as managing attorney, supervising the direct service work of the organization and assisting in the advocacy work. She also worked at Legal Services of Greater Miami, as the directing attorney of the American Immigration Lawyers Association Pro Bono Project, and at the Haitian Refugee Center, as a staff attorney. She clerked for a Florida state appellate court after graduating from the University of Florida Law School. She was born in Havana, Cuba, and raised in Florida.

Reviewer JANICE V. KAGUYUTAN is Senator Edward M. Kennedy's advisor on immigration, nationality, and refugee legislation and policies. Prior to working on Capitol Hill, Ms. Kaguyutan was a staff attorney at the NOW Legal Defense and Education Fund's Immigrant Women Program. Ms. Kaguyutan has written and trained extensively on the rights of immigrant victims of domestic violence, sexual assault, and human trafficking. Her previous work includes representing battered immigrant women in civil protection order, child support, divorce, and custody hearings, as well as representing immigrants before the Immigration and Naturalization Service on a variety of immigration matters.

JOE FERRY has been a writer and editor for 25 years, mostly in the newspaper industry. He lives in Perkasie, Pennsylvania, with his wife and three children. He has written books about the Vietnam Veterans Memorial, the Jefferson Memorial, the American Flag, and the National Anthem. Other book subjects include actress Helen Hunt and actor/director Rob Reiner.

PICTURE CREDITS